TUSCANY

Benedetta Geddo,
Mary Gray, Angelo Zinna

Meet our writers

Benedetta Geddo
@ *@beegeddo*

Born and raised in Italy, Benedetta has lived in France, Ireland, Poland and the US before returning to Piedmont where she is now based. Her work with Lonely Planet includes guides, news and feature pieces. She has two cats who are way too spoiled for their own good.

Mary Gray
@ *@verymarygray*

Mary's most in her element at a messy trattoria dinner. When not eating and drinking her way around Tuscany, you'll find her indulging her magpie impulses at antiques and vintage markets.

Angelo Zinna
@ *@angelo_zinna*

Angelo is a writer, editor and photographer based in Florence. Passionate about odd architecture, environment and the former Soviet region, he is the author of the book *Un Altro Bicchiere di Arak* (VME, 2016) and the podcast *Cemento*. His favorite experience is tackling an Apuan Alps (p206) trail with friends after a week spent on the keyboard.

Above Baccio Bandinelli's *Ercole e Caco* outside Palazzo Vecchio (p45), Florence **Previous spread** Siena (p74)

Contents

Montalcino, Montepulciano

Saturnia

STEVANZZ/GETTY IMAGES ©

Artimino

Vineyard, Castellina in Chianti (p83)

WOMEN ARTISTS

The Uffizi is dominated by works produced by male artists – Artemisia Gentileschi, Arcangela Paladini, Marietta Robusti are rare exceptions – but it is thought that thousands of women artists have gone unrecognised or been forgotten in Italy over the years.

FLORENTINE ART
JOURNEYS

Between the 14th and 17th centuries, Florence functioned as a magnet for painters, sculptors and architects who professed the return of the great classical arts and philosophy. The city remains one of the world's most impressive testaments of the artistic golden age known as the Renaissance, thanks to its endless collection of timeless artworks that captivate anyone who chooses to visit.

Left *The Birth of Venus* by Sandro Botticelli, Uffizi Gallery (p46) **Right** *David* by Michelangelo, Galleria dell'Accademia (p49) **Below** *Apoteosi di Cosimo I* by Giorgio Vasari, Palazzo Vecchio (p45)

→ THE DAVID

Many copies of the *David* are scattered around Florence, but nothing beats the first view of Michelangelo's original masterpiece in the Galleria dell'Accademia (p49).

THE BIRTH OF VENUS

The Birth of Venus by Sandro Botticelli is often considered the centrepiece of the Uffizi, although the competition is fierce with Leonardo da Vinci, Caravaggio, Piero della Francesca and Giotto all exhibited nearby.

↑ APOTEOSI DI COSIMO I

Giorgio Vasari's circular *Apoteosi di Cosimo I* placed at the centre of the Salone dei Cinquecento's marvellous ceiling shows Cosimo I de' Medici, Tuscany's first Grand Duke, in a heavenly scene.

Best Florentine Museum Experiences

▶ See one of the world's most precious art collections at the Uffizi Gallery. (p46)

▶ Admire Michelangelo's marble sculptures, including the glorious *David*, in the Galleria dell'Accademia. (p49)

▶ Gaze up at massive frescoes in Palazzo Vecchio's Salone dei Cinquecento. (p45)

▶ Find Donatello's heritage at the Museo del Bargello. (p49)

▶ Wander lush greenery with fountains and grottoes in the Giardino di Boboli. (p65)

Approximately 35 million bottles of Chianti Classico are produced each year in the provinces of Florence and Siena.

Some of Italy's most expensive wines are made in Tuscany; rare vintages of Brunello di Montalcino and Sassicaia can cost thousands per bottle.

There are nearly 65,000 hectares of vineyards in Tuscany.

IN VINO
VERITAS

If we are to believe – as the Latin saying goes – that with wine comes truth, your wisdom will multiply as you cross Tuscany north to south. Chianti is the big name here but as you'll soon discover, the region's rolling hills offer an exceptionally diverse sipping experience. From Bolgheri's Super Tuscans to Maremma's Morellino di Scansano, you'll never have to travel far to get to your next toast.

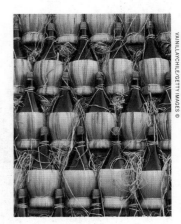

→ HITTING THE FIASCO

Chianti's infamous signature bottle – the *fiasco* – first appeared around the 13th century, when containers began to be covered by a layer of straw to protect the glass during transportation.

Left Vineyard, Castellina in Chianti (p83) **Right** *Fiaschi* (traditional Chianti bottles) **Below** Castello di Verrazzano

GAIOLE IN CHIANTI

A short drive from Florence is the small town of Gaiole in Chianti (p83), in the heart of the Chianti Classico region. Stop here to taste some of the area's best-known labels.

↑ CASTLE-HOPPING

Many of Tuscany's best-known wineries – such as the Castello di Verrazzano and the Castello di Meleto – are housed in grandiose castles once belonging to noble families who ruled the land.

Best Wine Experiences

▶ Search Tuscany's Strade del Vino (wine roads) for the best wines. (p174)

▶ Splurge on a bottle of Tenuta San Guido Sassicaia, one of the best-known Super Tuscan wines. (p180)

▶ Stop for a tasting in one of the charming hamlets of the Colli Senesi. (p83)

▶ Explore Morellino di Scansano, Chianti's lesser-known cousin, deep in Maremma. (p147)

There are over 4000 registered *agriturismi* operating in Tuscany's countryside – more than anywhere else in Italy.

There are more than 200 medieval castles and fortifications spread around the region.

SCENIC DRIVES
& HISTORY

There's no better way to fully experience the Tuscan riches than by driving through its twisting countryside roads. Picturesque hilltop hamlets, enchanting *agriturismi* (farm stays) and glorious landscapes come together once you exit the larger art cities, offering a mesmerising view of the region from an ever-changing perspective. Hit the road in spring or early summer to explore Tuscany in full bloom.

VYHA/GETTY IMAGES ©

→ THE LITTLE JERUSALEM

Wonderful Pitigliano (p138), known as the Little Jerusalem because of the Jewish community that once inhabited the area, appears above a natural stage made of tuff rock as you drive, turn after turn, through the area known as the Città del Tufo.

Left Viale dei Cipressi (p164)
Right Pitigliano (p138) **Below** Pecorino, Pienza

MEDIEVAL GEM

Views hardly get any better than those from welcoming Barga (p215), a quintessentially medieval village located in the heart of Garfagnana.

RIGHT: TANIA ZBROOKO/SHUTTERSTOCK ©
LEFT: STEVANZZ/SHUTTERSTOCK ©

↑ MOUTHWATERING PIENZA

With just over 2000 inhabitants, tiny Pienza (p112) is an exquisite break in your Val d'Orcia road trip, especially if you choose to stop for a plate of *pici* (a type of hand-rolled pasta) or a tasting of its famous *pecorino* cheese.

Best Road Trip Experiences

▶ Head to the ancient Città del Tufo atop towering rock formations amid forests. (p140)

▶ Explore the charming medieval cities of mountainous Garfagnana. (p214)

▶ Drive by towering cypresses on the pretty Viale dei Cipressi on your way to Bolgheri. (p164)

▶ Cut through romantic Val d'Orcia in search of the perfect sunset. (p118)

▶ Day-trip from Florence to the magnificent San Gimignano and Volterra. (p92)

Best Archaeology Experiences

► Reach the Etruscan city of Populonia overlooking the Tyrrhenian Sea. (p177)

► Cross into Maremma to check out the monumental tombs in the necropolis of Vetulonia. (p143)

► Admire an early Etruscan urban settlement at the Roselle archaeological park. (p143)

► Walk through the deep and narrow *vie cave* in Sovana in the Città del Tufo. (p141)

► Visit the remains of a legendary Etruscan settlement at the Cortona archaeological park. (p231)

PAOLO TROVO/SHUTTERSTOCK ©

A LOST
CIVILISATION

▬▬▬ The still-puzzling Etruscan people lived in a region formerly known as Etruria from approximately 900 BCE to the end of the millennia, when the Romans absorbed much of Tuscany into their territory. Dig deep into the layers of history by exploring the many undeciphered traces of this ancient civilisation that remain visible to this day.

CULINARY
TRADITION

Tuscany's diverse geography creates the perfect conditions for a satisfying gastronomic journey. From the hearty chestnut delicacies of the mountainous north to the truffle-covered pastas of the central hills and the seafood of the coast, the region's rich culinary landscape makes every day an opportunity to dig in to a mouthwatering meal.

Best Tuscan Food Experiences

▶ **Bite into a stuffed** *schiacciata* **sandwich in Florence.** (p68)

▶ **Take in Livorno's traditional** *cacciucco.* (p160)

▶ **Taste San Miniato's white truffle in autumn.** (p212)

▶ **Indulge in a sweet** *sfratto* **cake in Pitigliano.** (p139)

▶ **Warm up with the nutritious** *acquacotta* **(vegetable soup) in Maremma.** (p152)

TUSCANY BEST EXPERIENCES

TOP: LEONORI/GETTY IMAGES ©, BOTTOM: LUCHEZAR/GETTY IMAGES ©

→ CACCIUCCO ALLA LIVORNESE

Take octopus, mussels and other freshly caught sea creatures, cook them in tomato sauce, herbs and spices and serve with toasted *pane toscano* and olive oil – here's your Mediterranean postcard to devour.

← TAGLIOLINI AL TARTUFO

Proudly prepared in the medieval hamlet of San Miniato, *tagliolini* pasta served with locally hunted white or black truffle and Parmesan will have your taste buds trembling.

Opposite page Etruscan ruins, Roselle (p143)
Above left *Tagliolini al tartufo*
Left *Cacciucco*

SEASIDE
ESCAPES

■■■ You may not picture Tuscany as a beach destination, but its long coastline and seven-island archipelago are here to make you think again. Summer is when the seaside comes to life – perhaps excessively – but late spring and early autumn are excellent opportunities to discover the Tyrrhenian Sea in relative peace. Swim, snorkel, surf or sunbathe to your liking.

BRUNTIAGIO/GETTY IMAGES ©, BOTTOM: AURALAURA/SHUTTERSTOCK ©

★ BEACHSIDE HISTORY

Not far from its pristine coves, the island of Pianosa features some impressive Roman ruins that are worth visiting between sun-soaking sessions.

Best Swimming Experiences

▶ Dip your toes into the waters of Vada, near Livorno. (p167)

▶ Ride the waves in Cecina. (p167)

▶ Try some off-season snorkelling in Cala del Gesso, Monte Argentario. (p151)

▶ Relax on the wild beaches of Marina di Alberese, surrounded by a lush nature reserve. (p137)

← PELAGOS SANCTUARY FOR CETACEANS

There's more to the islands than sandy beaches and crystal-clear waters: whales, dolphins, turtles and manta rays have all made the Tuscan Archipelago their home.

Above left Dolphin, Pelagos Sanctuary for Cetaceans (p189)
Left Marina di Alberese (p137)
Above right Apuan Alps (p206)

Over 25% of Tuscany's surface is mountains. Monte Prado is the highest peak, at 2054m above sea level.

Approximately 7000km of hiking trails managed by the CAI (Italian Alpine Club) in Tuscany.

Best Hiking Experiences

▶ Discover the wild landscapes of the rugged yet fragile ecosystem of the Apuan Alps. (p206)

▶ Walk the Via Francigena, an ancient pilgrim route cutting through the region and stretching all the way to Rome and eventually Jerusalem. (p210)

▶ Hike the Apennines in the Parco Nazionale delle Foreste Casentinesi, on the border between Tuscany and Emilia-Romagna. (p232)

▶ Explore the lush Parco Regionale della Maremma for close encounters with the local wildlife. (p134)

PHOTOFRA/SHUTTERSTOCK ©

HIKING
ADVENTURES

▬▬▬ The extreme abundance of culture, history and good food makes it way too easy to sit back and enjoy all the life pleasures Tuscany has on offer, but forgetting about the great outdoors means missing out on endless opportunities to experience the region at its rawest. Turn your trip into an active adventure by hitting the trails far from the crowds.

● Pistoia

● Pescia   **Montecatini
Terme** ●

Prato ●

*Lago di
Massaciuccoli*

Lucca ●

*Parco Regionale
Migliarino San
Rossore Massaciuccoli*

● **Pisa**

● Cascina

● **Pontedera**

● **Ponsacco**

**San
Gimignano**
●

Piazza dell'Anfiteatro
Lucca's unique main square

Echoing the structure of the 2nd-century Roman
amphitheatre once found in the city, Lucca's main
square is unique in its elliptical shape. Irregular,
yellow buildings enclose the piazza and the outdoor
seating areas of its restaurant – beyond them, a long
list of medieval masterpieces await within Lucca's
perfectly preserved city walls.

🚗 *50mins from Barga*

▶ p204

Piazza dei Miracoli
Pisa's miracle square

Although most people think of the Leaning
Tower as a quick photo stop on the way to
elsewhere, Pisa's 'miracle square' is worth
at least a few hours of your time. The
cathedral dedicated to Santa Maria
Assunta, the baptistery and the cemetery
spread on the grassy field of Piazza dei
Miracoli are just some of the remnants of
the glorious maritime power.

🚆 *1hr from Florence*

▶ p196

INIMITABLE
PIAZZAS

▬▬ No Italian city would be complete without at
least one major square, and Tuscany has plenty of
wonderful piazzas welcoming visitors at the
crossroads of past and present. The piazza – heir of
the Greek *agorà* and the Roman *forum* – is where
urban life flourishes through politics, commerce,
public celebrations and art, today as yesterday.

SOUTHERN
TUSCANY

Piazza del Duomo, Pistoia
Pistoia's overlooked highlights

Once an influential medieval commune, Pistoia doesn't make it to most traveller itineraries despite being a worthy day trip from Florence. Its Piazza del Duomo, home to the 13th-century Cattedrale di San Zeno and the 14th-century Battistero di San Giovanni, becomes a lively market every Wednesday and Saturday.

🚆 *40mins from Florence*
▶ p208

Sesto ●**Fiorentino**

Florence ●

Piazza del Duomo, Florence
Florence's hidden treasures

Filippo Brunelleschi's 116m-tall dome topping the majestic Santa Maria del Fiore cathedral marks the heart of the city with its red tiles. But in and around the symmetrical structure, built on the remains of the ancient Chiesa di Santa Reparata, more invaluable treasures lay hidden.

▶ p52

EASTERN TUSCANY

● **Poggibonsi**

CENTRAL TUSCANY

Arezzo ●

Riserva
Naturale
Alto Merse

 ●**Siena**

Piazza del Campo
Siena's medieval piazza

The semi-circular, sloping red square around which Siena is built is known as one of the great medieval Italian piazzas. It is here, under the shadow of the Palazzo Pubblico and the Torre del Mangia, that each year the Palio horse race has been held since the 17th century.

🚆 *1½hrs from Florence*
▶ p87

● **Asciano**

Piazza Grande
Vasari's Arezzo birthplace

Dating back to the early 13th century, the central square of Giorgio Vasari's place of birth features one of the Renaissance artist's most prominent architectural works: the Palazzo delle Logge, a 1573 structure recalling his earlier work in Florence.

🚆 *1½hrs from Florence*
▶ p226

 0 ▬▬▬ 20 km
0 ▬▬▬ 10 miles

→ Calcio Storico

In June Florence's Piazza Santa Croce turns into a sand arena where the brutal *calcio storico* (historic football) tournament takes place.
- Florence
- ▶ p62

↘ Firenze Rocks

Florence's largest park, the Cascine, hosts one of the region's biggest music festivals. Previous editions have welcomed Metallica, Red Hot Chili Peppers and Green Day.
- Florence
- ▶ firenzerocks.it

Luminaria di San Ranieri

Pisa's patron saint is celebrated on 16 June, with the city setting up thousands of candles on the banks of the Arno river, before the opening of a grandiose fireworks show.

↓ Pistoia Blues

Local and international stars draw crowds to Piazza del Duomo in July for a series of perfectly framed concerts.
- Pistoia
- ▶ pistoiablues.com

JUNE

Average daytime max: 28°C
Days of rainfall: 6

JULY

Tuscany in
SUMMER

← Lucca Summer Festival

Global stars of the pop and rock scenes come to Lucca in late July to transform the city into a huge music venue.

● Lucca

▶ luccasummerfestival.it

↓ Teatro del Silenzio

An orchestra accompanies tenor Andrea Bocelli and friends in the yearly concert held in Lajatico's natural amphitheatre.

● Lajatico

▶ teatrodelsilenzio.it

↙ Festival Puccini

Between July and August, Torre del Lago's open-air theatre hosts a festival dedicated to the great composer Giacomo Puccini, who lived in the seaside town most of his life.

● Torre del Lago

▶ puccinifestival.it

TUSCANY PLAN BY SEASON

Average daytime max: 31°C
Days of rainfall: 4

AUGUST

Average daytime max: 31°C
Days of rainfall: 5

← Palio di Siena

Siena's most awaited event takes place each year on 2 July and 16 August at Piazza del Campo, the city's main square.

● Siena

▶ p96

🧳 Packing Notes

August is the peak holiday season in Italy. Sunscreen and mosquito repellent are essential. Bring swimwear, hiking boots or your festival outfit depending on your interests.

As summer turns into autumn, wineries around the region get busy harvesting and processing grapes that will become one of Tuscany's prime exports.

↘ Expo del Chianti

Early September is when winemakers from the Chianti Classico region come together in Greve in Chianti to showcase their best bottles.
- Greve
- ▶ expochianticlassico.com

↓ L'Eroica

Gaiole in Chianti hosts the legendary L'Eroica bicycle race where athletes compete with vintage bikes on white roads in early October each year.
- Gaiole
- ▶ eroica.cc

Autumn is a beautiful season to see Tuscan nature changing colours. Visit the Franciscan Sanctuary of La Verna in the Apennines or Monte Amiata for awe-inspiring views.

SEPTEMBER

Average daytime max: 26°C
Days of rainfall: 7

OCTOBER

Tuscany in
AUTUMN

Many towns – including Marradi, San Gimignano and Monte Amiata – celebrate the chestnut harvest with mouthwatering festivals in October.

→ Lucca Comics & Games

One of Europe's largest comics festivals attracts cosplayers from all over to the medieval town of Lucca in early November.

📍 Lucca

▶ luccacomicsandgames.com

↑ Terre di Pisa Food & Wine Festival

Producers of wine, olive oil, cheese and other artisanal edibles meet in Pisa's Piazza Vittorio Emanuele II in mid-October to celebrate and promote the local culinary heritage.

📍 Pisa

▶ terredipisa.it

Average daytime max: 21°C
Days of rainfall: 9

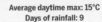

Average daytime max: 15°C
Days of rainfall: 9

NOVEMBER

↙ Mostra Mercato del Tartufo Bianco

San Miniato hosts a festival dedicated to its most precious product – white truffle – each year in November.

📍 San Miniato

▶ p114

🧳 Packing Notes

Evenings get chilly as summer fades out. Bring an extra layer of clothing, a raincoat and comfortable shoes.

↓ Christmas Markets

Many cities – including Florence, Pisa, Lucca and Livorno – set up Christmas markets in the weeks leading up to the holiday.

← Firenze Light Festival

In December and January many iconic Florentine buildings become canvases for grand, colourful light installations that adorn the city for more than a month.
📍 Florence
▶ p61

← New Year Celebrations

Florence usually hosts a series of open-air concerts on 31 December, followed by fireworks that inaugurate the New Year.
📍 Florence

DECEMBER

Average daytime min: 3°C
Days of rainfall: 7

JANUARY

Tuscany in
WINTER

← Festa di Anna Maria de' Medici

To thank the last member of the Medici family for gifting Florence with an invaluable cultural heritage, the city holds a parade and offers free admission to many museums in February.
📍 Florence

Befana

On 6 January, an old woman known in Italian folklore as the Befana is said to visit children to fill their socks with candy or charcoal depending on their past behaviour.

← Disfida dei Falò

An ancient tradition is kept alive in Pontremoli, where two parishes compete in building the biggest fire – which can reach up to 30m high – on 17 and 31 January.
📍 Pontremoli

Average daytime min: 3°C
Days of rainfall: 6

FEBRUARY

Average daytime min: 3°C
Days of rainfall: 6

Winter is ski time – head to Abetone for a day or two on the slopes.

← Carnevale di Viareggio

Early February is not the best time to head to the coast – unless we're talking about Viareggio, where huge Carnival parades take place.
📍 Viareggio
▶ p217

 Packing Notes

Bring a heavy jacket, gloves and waterproof shoes – it can get rainy.

From March onwards, restaurant menus become filled with dishes cooked with two springtime favourites: asparagus and artichokes

← Scoppio del Carro

On Easter Sunday a 500-year-old, firework-filled cart is brought to the front of the Duomo in Florence by 150 soldiers in traditional costumes and ignited by the cardinal to wish the city a plentiful spring season.

📍 Florence

↓ Lavender Blooms

As spring rolls into summer, the lavender fields of Santa Luce, south of Pisa, turn violet creating a unique natural spectacle.

MARCH

Average daytime max: 15°C
Days of rainfall: 7

APRIL

Tuscany in
SPRING

↘ Balestro del Girifalco

One of Tuscany's prime medieval reenactments is held in May in Massa Marittima, where archers from three rival neighbourhoods compete shooting a target with 15th-century crossbows.

● Massa Marittima

↑ Maggio Musicale Fiorentino

Opera lovers will want to plan their trip between April and June, when a long list of shows are performed in the city's main theatre. View the full program online.

● Florence

▶ maggiofiorentino.com

TUSCANY PLAN BY SEASON

Average daytime max: 19°C
Days of rainfall: 8

MAY

Average daytime max: 24°C
Days of rainfall: 7

Packing Notes

While mostly sunny, weather can vary greatly in spring – best to layer up. Bring a light rain jacket and a jumper for chilly evenings.

ART CITIES
Trip Builder

TAKE YOUR PICK OF MUST-SEES AND HIDDEN GEMS

▬▬▬ Even if you're short on time or would rather not confront Italian traffic from behind the wheel, there are many possible day trips from Florence that will allow you to delve deeper into the region's culture and history.

🗺 Trip Notes

Hub town Florence

How long 7–10 days

Getting around No hassle – all of the listed destinations are easily reached by train as day or weekend trips from Florence. Buy tickets online at trenitalia.com.

Tips Florence's three train stations often confuse first-time visitors: Santa Maria Novella is the central station. High-speed Le Frecce and Italo trains often offer discounts on weekends.

Pistoia
A short train ride from Florence leads to the heart of charming Pistoia, a historic centre dotted with Romanesque architecture hiding precious artworks.
🚆 *40mins from Florence*

● Pisa

● Cascina

● Pontedera

Lucca
Dedicate a full day to welcoming Lucca, where you'll find stunning architecture, a lively town centre and great art all locked within the walkable 16th-century walls.
🚆 *1hr 20mins from Florence*

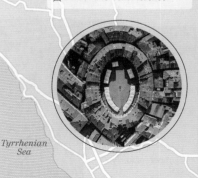

Tyrrhenian Sea

Serchio

```
     0                    10 km
 ⓝ   0              5 miles
```

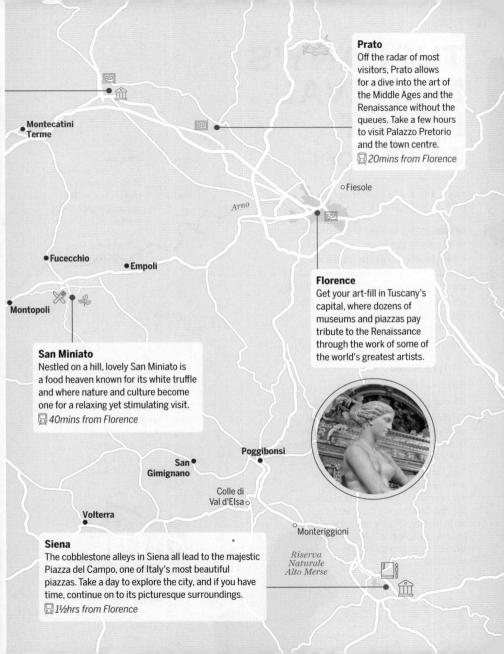

Montecatini Terme

Prato

Off the radar of most visitors, Prato allows for a dive into the art of the Middle Ages and the Renaissance without the queues. Take a few hours to visit Palazzo Pretorio and the town centre.

🚆 *20mins from Florence*

○ Fiesole

Arno

● **Fucecchio**   ● **Empoli**

● **Montopoli**

Florence

Get your art-fill in Tuscany's capital, where dozens of museums and piazzas pay tribute to the Renaissance through the work of some of the world's greatest artists.

San Miniato

Nestled on a hill, lovely San Miniato is a food heaven known for its white truffle and where nature and culture become one for a relaxing yet stimulating visit.

🚆 *40mins from Florence*

San Gimignano ●

Poggibonsi ●

Colle di Val d'Elsa ○

Volterra ●

○ Monteriggioni

Siena

The cobblestone alleys in Siena all lead to the majestic Piazza del Campo, one of Italy's most beautiful piazzas. Take a day to explore the city, and if you have time, continue on to its picturesque surroundings.

🚆 *1½hrs from Florence*

Riserva Naturale Alto Merse

TUSCANY'S MEDIEVAL HEART
Trip Builder

TAKE YOUR PICK OF MUST-SEES AND HIDDEN GEMS

Travel inland from the coast to discover stone-built medieval cities where powerful families once fought each other from their *case torri* (tower houses), then continue on to discover abandoned Gothic cathedrals and quaint hamlets nestled in the sun-soaked hilly countryside.

🗺 Trip Notes

Hub towns Pisa, Volterra, Siena

How long 14 days

Getting around Pick up your rental car when you land in Pisa and drive patiently through the *strade normali* rather than the motorway for the best optical effect.

Tips The season dictates many of the possible detours on this itinerary. In warmer months you could opt to drive the first stretch along the coast for a dip in the sea along the way, otherwise consider making quick stops in Pontedera, Montescudaio and Lajatico on your way to Volterra.

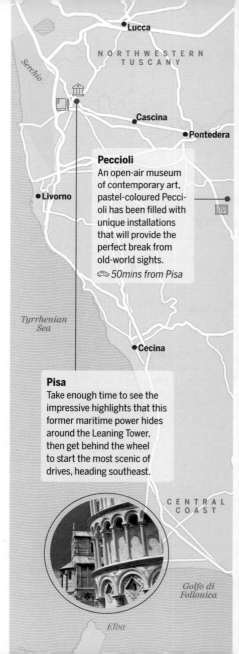

Lucca

NORTHWESTERN TUSCANY

Serchio

Cascina

Pontedera

Peccioli
An open-air museum of contemporary art, pastel-coloured Peccioli has been filled with unique installations that will provide the perfect break from old-world sights.
🚗 *50mins from Pisa*

Livorno

Tyrrhenian Sea

Cecina

Pisa
Take enough time to see the impressive highlights that this former maritime power hides around the Leaning Tower, then get behind the wheel to start the most scenic of drives, heading southeast.

CENTRAL COAST

Golfo di Follonica

Elba

San Gimignano

The 'City of 72 Towers' no longer stands up to its nickname (only 13 are left), but the Unesco-listed centre remains an impressive sight, especially if you admire it while holding an award-winning Dondoli gelato.

🚗 50mins from Siena

Arno

• **Florence**

Riserva Naturale Vallombrosa

EASTERN TUSCANY

Monteriggioni

A tiny hilltop fortification surrounded by vineyards and olive groves, located right on the ancient Via Francigena pilgrimage route.

🚗 25mins from Siena

Poggibonsi

Castellina in Chianti

Gaiole in Chianti

Colle di Val d'Elsa

Siena

Plan a break from charming hamlets in lively Siena, where next to exceptional architecture you'll find a vast selection of top-quality eateries and artisanal souvenir shopping opportunities.

🚗 1hr from Volterra

Volterra

Volterra's double-walled urban plan surrounding the central Palazzo dei Priori echoes its Etruscan origins but has its roots deep in the Middle Ages.

🚗 1hr 15mins from Pisa

Riserva Naturale Alto Merse

CENTRAL TUSCANY

Abbazia di San Galgano

In the middle of the Senese countryside, near the sleepy village of Chiusdino, is the now-abandoned 13th-century San Galgano Abbey, a spectacular, roofless church with an intriguing history.

🚗 40mins from Siena

Montalcino •

• **Pienza**

Val d'Orcia

Rightly stereotypical images of Tuscany come to life in Val d'Orcia where sun-kissed hills embrace dozens of quaint settlements just waiting to be framed.

🚗 1hr from Siena

SOUTHERN TUSCANY

0 20 km
0 10 miles

THE MAREMMA
Trip Builder

TAKE YOUR PICK OF MUST-SEES AND HIDDEN GEMS

Tuscany's 400km coastline offers more than sandy beaches in family-friendly seaside towns. Head into the heart of the Maremma to explore Etruscan relics, overlooked art cities and an untamed wilderness that is the region's first natural reserve.

🗺 Trip Notes

Hub towns Livorno, Massa Marittima, Grosseto

How long 14 days

Getting around Maremma occupies roughly 25% of Tuscany's mainland, stretching from Cecina all the way to Lazio. Start your trip in Livorno following the coastline and make frequent inland detours to check out some of the region's best-kept secrets.

Tips Maremma is home to the Morellino di Scansano wine region. Wineries typically open up to visitors from spring to autumn, making countryside deviations even more worth it. Plenty of *agriturismi* (farm stays) are available in the area.

Tyrrhenian Sea

CENTRAL COAST

Bolgheri
Known to the world for its Super Tuscan wines made from non-indigenous grape varieties, Bolgheri is an obligatory tasting stop for any vino lover.
🚗 *50mins from Livorno*

Cecina●

San Vincenzo○

Piombino○

Populonia
Etruscan relics face the open sea in the ancient city of Populonia. If time and weather allow, consider a trip to the Isola d'Elba from the nearby port of Piombino.
🚗 *1hr 15mins from Livorno*

Pianosa

Ⓝ 0 — 20 km
0 — 10 miles

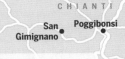

Livorno
After feasting on delicious *cacciucco* (mixed seafood stew) in the coastal city of Livorno, it's time to get driving to reach the southernmost tip of Tuscany.

CHIANTI

San Gimignano   Poggibonsi

Montevarchi

Massa Marittima
Head inland to visit the gracious medieval centre of Massa Marittima, where the refined 11th-century Cattedrale di San Cerbone hosts some of Giovanni Pisano's most beautiful sculptures.
🚗 *1hr 20mins from Livorno*

Città del Tufo
Pitigliano, Sovana and Sorano (pictured) form the area known as the Città del Tufo, where stunning cities built on top of volcanic rock formations have been inhabited since Etruscan times.
🚗 *1hr 20mins from Grosseto*

Riserva Naturale Alto Merse

Parco Regionale della Maremma
Diversity is what makes Maremma so great, and you'll hardly find a more varied ecosystem than in this nature reserve. Thick forests, beaches, birds, ruins and long-standing farming traditions come together to form a delicate yet fascinating environment.
🚗 *15mins from Grosseto*

Castel del Piano

○ Follonica

Golfo di Follonica

TUSCANY

Capalbio
The hilltop hamlet offers unbeatable views on the Tyrrhenian coast, but for a truly unique sight head to the nearby Giardino dei Tarocchi (Tarot Gardens) where French-American artist Niki de Saint Phalle created a mind-expanding sculpture park.
🚗 *45mins from Grosseto*

Riserva Naturale Provinciale Diaccia Botrona

Grosseto

● Pitigliano

LAZIO

Vetulonia
The Etruscan necropolis makes a worthy stop on the way back to the coast, thanks to its monumental tombs that have remained intact for 2500 years.
🚗 *30mins from Grosseto*

Porto Santo Stefano

● Orbetello

Monte Argentario

Giglio

THE WILD NORTH
Trip Builder

TAKE YOUR PICK OF MUST-SEES AND HIDDEN GEMS

▬▬▬ The northern, mountainous edge of Tuscany offers many high-altitude hiking opportunities among the sharp peaks and grassy valleys of the Apuan Alps and the Apennines. But the Garfagnana and the Lunigiana areas have more than the outdoors to offer – a culture made of great food, wine and history welcomes those who choose the less-beaten track.

🗺️ Trip Notes

Hub towns Lucca, Castelnuovo di Garfagnana

How long 12–14 days

Getting around While public transport does reach the main urban centres of northwestern Tuscany, driving remains the most effective way to explore, especially if you're planning to visit remote natural sights. Lucca is the best place to start your journey.

Tip Break your journey by booking a relaxing farm stay anywhere around Castelnuovo di Garfagnana or Barga.

Vagli
Endless trails start from Vagli, where a lake now covers the lost city of Fabbriche di Careggine. Don't miss a visit to Campocatino.
🚗 *40mins from Castelnuovo di Garfagnana*

Carrara

Parco Naturale delle Alpi Apuane

Colonnata
Cross the Apuan Alps to reach the tiny town known for its *lardo* (cured fatback) and marble production. Take a long mountain hike to the David mural by Brazilian street artist Eduardo Kobra at 850m altitude.
🚗 *1hr 20mins from Lucca*

Seravezza

Pietrasanta
After much hiking, head back to the coast for a well-deserved break in the artistic hub of Pietrasanta, just 3km from the sandy Versilian beaches.
🚗 *40mins from Lucca*

Marina di Pietrasanta

Lido di Camaiore

```
0        5 km
0      2.5 miles
```

Mediterranean Sea

Campocatino

Careggine

Lago di Vagli

Pieve Fosciana

Lago di Pontecosi

Castelnuovo di Garfagnana

Garfagnana's main hub offers endless opportunities for both adrenaline seekers and extreme relaxation enthusiasts.

🚗 *1hr from Lucca*

N O R T H W E S T E R N
T U S C A N Y

Garfagnana

Barga

The rustic atmosphere of this charming little hamlet blends with the undomesticated nature of the surrounding woods – recharge your batteries in one of the nearby farm stays.

🚗 *50mins from Lucca*

Fornaci di Barga

Lucignano

Calavorno

Fornovolasco

Isola Santa

Time seems to have stopped in this magical *borgo* (hamlet), comprising a few dozen houses with slab stone roofs overlooking an artificial lake.

🚗 *20mins from Castelnuovo di Garfagnana*

Borgo a Mozzano

Make a quick stop in the isolated town known for its paper production to admire the 11th-century Devil's Bridge, allegedly built by Satan himself.

🚗 *30mins from Lucca*

Serchio

Vinchiana

Monsagrati

Lucca

Start off in the medieval city of Lucca, the gateway to the Garfagnana, then head north on the SS12 before turning left to follow the Serchio River.

Torre del Lago

Lago di Massaciuccoli

7 Things to Know About **TUSCANY**

INSIDER TIPS TO HIT THE GROUND RUNNING

1 For Transport Tickets, Think Ahead

Never hop on a bus, train or tram expecting to purchase a ticket on board – since the Covid-19 pandemic, the option to pay cash for a bus ticket through the driver's window has been eliminated, and the already-rare, on-board cashless ticket kiosks, virtually so. Instead, look for *edicole* (newsstands), tobacconists, supermarkets and bars bearing the 'AT' vendor logo – Autolinee Toscane (at-bus.it) is the local transport authority across Tuscany. Once on board remember to timestamp your tickets by inserting them in the designated machines.

4 Take Coffee at the Bar

Payment procedures at a Tuscan bar-cafe can feel like pandemonium. If in doubt: when it's busy, order at the till then take your receipt to the barista. When it's just you and one or two other customers, you can safely head to the bar first. In most bars, remember you'll pay a slight-to-significant markup for drinking your coffee while seated (*a tavolo*) versus standing at the bar (*al banco*).

2 Dress Decently

Most Tuscans veer classic-chic in their dress, and conservative, well-tailored clothing in neutral fabrics is the norm. You'll blend in better if you steer clear of workout clothing, loud logos and flip-flops.

3 Monday Closures

Most state-run cultural sites and museums, plus others that fall outside that category, are closed on Mondays, as are shops and various services.

5 Covid-19 Situation

Having lived through one of the world's toughest lockdowns, Tuscans are still comparatively cautious about Covid-19. Though most mandates have been lifted, FFP2 (KN95) masks are still widely available and used. The most authoritative and up-to-date source for Covid-related restrictions is the Ministry of Health website (salute.gov.it/travellers).

6 Have a Laugh

Tuscans are both spirited and world-weary. Humour here is ironic and sly, with colourful slang and curse words aplenty, suspicion toward the politically correct and a penchant for wordplay. Shopkeepers might seem a bit brusque to those with more reserved sensibilities – don't be alarmed if jokes and pleasantries don't always land well in English.

7 Local Lingo

Here are a few words to get you started talking to Tuscans on your trip.

Grazie Thank you.

Prego A wonderful word with different situational meanings. It's the standard response to *'grazie',* but can also be an invitation to act. *Prego* can mean something akin to 'go ahead' (a barista uses it to signal that they're ready to take your order) or 'after you' (the person ahead of you in the supermarket queue notices your near-empty cart and politely calls you forward).

Hoha-Hola A tongue-in-cheek, local in-joke illustrating how native Tuscans, particularly Florentines, would typically pronounce Coca-Cola. The regional tendency to switch out the hard 'c' sound with an 'h' sound is a linguistic quirk to keep in mind, whether you're ordering coffee or corporate soda.

Semaforo Traffic light – a tough-to-guess word that crops up often when generous locals offer directions.

▶ For more on language, see p250

Read, Listen, Watch & Follow

 READ

The Stones of Florence (Mary McCarthy; 1959)
History and snappy social commentary about the Renaissance city and its residents.

The Merchant of Prato (Iris Origo; 1957)
Medieval life in a now-industrial Tuscan town is explored through the life of Francesco di Marco Datini.

The Decameron
(Giovanni Boccaccio; c 1349–51) One hundred stories narrated by young adventurers who flee Florence to the hills amid the plague.

Florence in Ecstasy
(Jessie Chaffee; 2017) A young American healing from an eating disorder develops a fascination with ascetic female saints.

 LISTEN

Cooking with an Italian Accent
(Giulia Scarpaleggia) Acclaimed food writer shares stories, food lore and recipes from her Tuscan countryside home.

Jovanotti for President
(Jovanotti; 1988) Panned by critics, but sung by an enduring Cortona-raised pop singer (pictured), this album came to be associated with the vapidity of youth culture in the '80s.

Ciao Bella (Erica Firpo)
Rome-based travel writer interviews the people shaping Italian culture today; find episodes on Florence and Tuscany.

Se mi rilasso collasso
(Bandabardò) Deceptively breezy

tune from Florence-born folk band, whose leader Erriquez was outspoken about his city's treatment of its musicians.

El Diablo (Litfiba)
Rock-tinged album from one of Florence's native bands, with strong ties to the San Niccolò neighbourhood.

▷ **WATCH**

A Room with a View (James Ivory; 1985)
The British romance that launched many
love affairs with Florence.
Romeo and Juliet (Franco Zeffirelli; 1968;
pictured top right) Zeffirelli's take on the
classic features key scenes in Pienza.
Amici miei (Mario Monicelli; 1975; pictured
bottom right) Five Florentine friends confront
middle age in a less romanticised Florence.
Tea with Mussolini (Franco Zeffirelli; 1999)
A semi-autobiographical film about an
Italian boy raised during WWII by a group of
American and English women.
Life Is Beautiful (Roberto Benigni; 1997)
Oscar-winning comedy drama about a
Jewish family from Arezzo set during WWII.

◎ **FOLLOW**

@danielerossichef
Join the huge online
following of affable
Tuscan chef Daniele
Rossi.

visittuscany.com
@VisitTuscany
Official tourism
account with activities
and cultural sites by
category.

The Florentine
(theflorentine.net)
News and lifestyle outlet
with event listings.

The Week in Italy
(theweekinitaly.
substack.com) Weekly
roundup of Italian
news and culture.

**@creativepeople
inflorence**
A showcase of the
city's contemporary
designers, artisans
and artists.

FLORENCE

CULTURE | ART | HISTORY

Experience
Florence
online

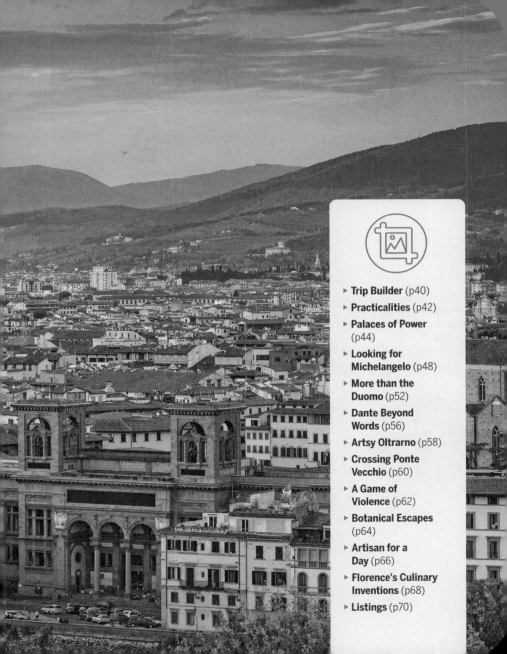

FLORENCE
Trip Builder

Explore opulent palaces and museums overflowing with extraordinary paintings and sculptures, then climb to romantic terraces offering exceptional views of the red rooftops. Allow plenty of time to get lost in the city's narrow alleys and you'll likely be asking yourself when you'll return.

Stazione di Santa Maria Novella

Visit the art-filled rooms of **Palazzo Pitti**, one of the Medici's most sumptuous residences (p47)
🚶 *5mins from Ponte Vecchio*

PIGNONE

Explore the hidden gems of **San Frediano**, the working-class neighbourhood turned creative hub (p58)
🚶 *10mins from Ponte Vecchio*

Ponte Amerigo Vespucci

Via Pisana

Lungarno Soderini

Ponte alla Carraia

Lungarno Corsini

Borgo San Frediano

Ponte Santa Trinita

Via di Santo Spirito

Via de' Tornabuoni

Via Faenza

MONTICELLI

Piazza Torquato Tasso

SANTO SPIRITO

Stop for an *aperitivo* at the lively **Piazza Santo Spirito** in the Oltrarno area across the river (p59)
🚶 *6mins from Ponte Vecchio*

Viale Francesco Petrarca

Giardino Torrigiani

Via de' Serragli

Via Maggio

Via Romana

Via della Meridiana

BELLOSGUARDO

Walk among monumental fountains in central Florence's green lung, the **Giardino di Boboli** (p65)
🚶 *5mins from Ponte Vecchio*

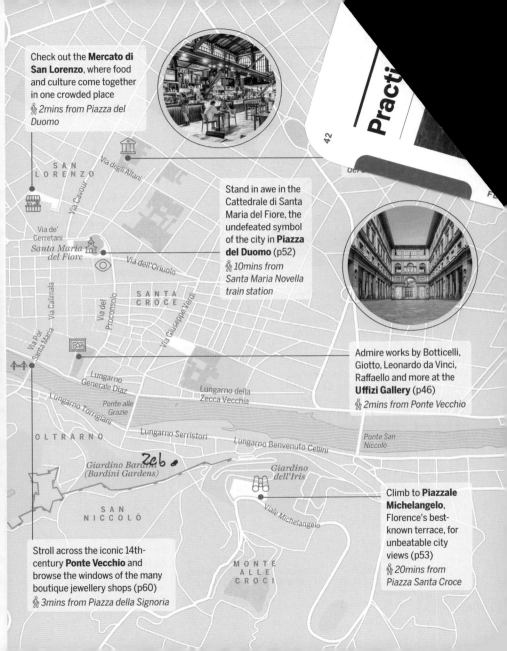

Check out the **Mercato di San Lorenzo**, where food and culture come together in one crowded place

🚶 *2mins from Piazza del Duomo*

Stand in awe in the Cattedrale di Santa Maria del Fiore, the undefeated symbol of the city in **Piazza del Duomo** (p52)

🚶 *10mins from Santa Maria Novella train station*

Admire works by Botticelli, Giotto, Leonardo da Vinci, Raffaello and more at the **Uffizi Gallery** (p46)

🚶 *2mins from Ponte Vecchio*

Climb to **Piazzale Michelangelo**, Florence's best-known terrace, for unbeatable city views (p53)

🚶 *20mins from Piazza Santa Croce*

Stroll across the iconic 14th-century **Ponte Vecchio** and browse the windows of the many boutique jewellery shops (p60)

🚶 *3mins from Piazza della Signoria*

VITALYEDUSH/GETTY IMAGES ©

ARRIVING

Florence Airport (Aeroporto di Firenze-Peretola) Florence's main airport is located 6km from the city centre. The T2 tram connects the airport to Santa Maria Novella train station in about 25 minutes (tickets €1.50).

Santa Maria Novella SMN is Florence's central main train station, connected directly to most major cities in Italy via regional and high-speed rail services such as Freccia Rossa and Italo. From here, Piazza del Duomo is a 10-minute walk.

HOW MUCH FOR A

Small gelato
€2.50

Margherita pizza
€7

Negroni cocktail
€8

GETTING AROUND

Walking One trip is hardly enough to take in all that Florence has to offer, but its small area makes diving into the Renaissance heritage a joyful journey through some of the world's best art and architecture. Walking is the best way to get around the city centre.

Cycling Florence has a decent network of cycle paths circling the historic centre. The Ciclovia dell'Arno, a 270km cycling route running along the Arno river from its mouth in Stia to Pisa, was being developed at time of research with completion planned for late 2022.

Tram Three tram lines connect the city centre with the airport, the Careggi Hospital and nearby Scandicci, where long-distance coaches depart from the Villa Costanza bus station.

WHEN TO GO

JAN–MAR
The coldest time of the year, but also the least crowded.

APR–JUN
Warm sunny days with gardens in full bloom – a great season to visit.

JUL–SEP
The long, pleasant summer nights make up for the hot and humid days.

OCT–DEC
Temperatures cool down as the city prepares for the holiday season.

EATING & DRINKING

Reducing the local cuisine to the famous *bistecca alla fiorentina* – the thick T-bone Florentine steak served rare – is a mistake. Stuffed *schiacciata* (flat bread made with olive oil; pictured top), *pappa al pomodoro* (bread and tomato soup) and *ribollita* (a thick vegetable, bread and bean soup; pictured bottom) are just some of Florence's all-time classics made with just a few simple ingredients to be paired with a generous glass of Chianti. Looking for something fancier than a trattoria? Half a dozen Michelin-starred restaurants – including Massimo Bottura's new Gucci Osteria – dot the city serving modern reinventions of cult dishes.

| **Must-try *schiacciata*** | **Best trattoria** | **Best cocktails** |
| Sapori Toscani (p68) | Trattoria Guelfa (p72) | Locale (p73) |

CONNECT

Wi-fi Connect to the spotty yet functioning 'Firenze WiFi' network for up to 500MB of free data per day. Most cafes in the city will also offer free wi-fi to customers.

Data connection Due to the thick stone walls of some buildings, data connection can be poor when you are inside.

FIRENZECARD

The **Firenzecard** (firenzecard. it) costs €85 and allows access to 50-plus museums in the city for 72 hours. With the Firenzecard+ add-on (€7) you'll also get unlimited public transport for the same duration.

WHERE TO STAY

The historical centre is easily explored on foot, with major sights within reach from every neighbourhood. As the weather gets warmer some areas get louder in the evenings, as bar crowds spill onto the streets.

Neighbourhood	Pro/Con
Santa Maria Novella	Florence's main transit hub, easily reached from the airport and other cities by train.
Piazza del Duomo & Piazza della Signoria	This central area is great to explore the city; prices might be steep during high season.
Piazza Santa Croce	Close to the nightlife and all the main sights. Large student population.
San Frediano (Oltrarno)	Great restaurants and bars nearby. Lower prices than the northern side of the Arno.
Santo Spirito (Oltrarno)	Local feel and lovely market vibe. The piazza gets loud at night, especially during summer.
San Niccolò (Oltrarno)	Many luxurious homes dot this quiet yet upscale neighbourhood with great views.

MONEY

Credit cards are widely accepted, but some shops remain cash-only. Tipping is not expected unless the service offered is particularly personalised. Avoid restaurants where prices are not displayed.

01 Palaces of **POWER**

ART | ARCHITECTURE | MUSEUMS

No family has been as influential in the history of Florence as the Medici family. Ruling for over three centuries, the bankers turned politicians have shaped the city through grandiose palaces, vast art collections, refined gardens and opulent churches – immerse yourself in the Renaissance.

Above Palazzo Pitti
Right Fresco, Magi Chapel, Palazzo Medici Riccardi

ROBMENTING/SHUTTERSTOCK ©

FLORENCE EXPERIENCES

🗺 How to

Visiting Each museum requires a separate ticket unless you purchase the Firenzecard (p43), which allows access to all major sights for 72 hours.

When to go Go early in the morning to avoid crowds. Tickets for Palazzo Pitti are half price before 8.59am.

Final resting place
The Basilica di San Lorenzo (p50) was the Medici's official church. Here, in the Cappelle Medicee's Sagrestia Nuova, designed by Michelangelo, are the tombs of Lorenzo II Magnifico (Lorenzo de' Medici) and his brother Giuliano.

The Medici Family's First Residence

Commissioned by Cosimo the Elder in 1444, **Palazzo Medici Riccardi** has hosted many of the city's most prominent figures, including Lorenzo il Magnifico, Donatello, Michelangelo and Botticelli. Enter through Via Cavour 3 into the elegant Cortile di Michelozzo, named after the building's architect, then continue through the Medici Garden and the mesmerising Magi Chapel painted by Benedetto Gazzoli (1459). The Gallery Luca Giordano, a Baroque masterpiece added after the Riccardi family acquired the building (1659), contains the stunning ceiling fresco *Apoteosi dei Medici* (1685).

One of the City's Icons

Palazzo Vecchio has been Florence's political core for over seven centuries. Designed by Arnolfo di Cambio in 1299 to host the republic's functionaries, the palace became the Medici's residence in 1540, when the first Grand Duke of Tuscany Cosimo I moved in with his court. Visit the splendid **Salone dei Cinquecento**, where Renaissance masters Leonardo da Vinci and Michelangelo worked side by side on two large-scale, never-completed frescoes. Look up to see Giorgio Vasari's *Apoteosi di Cosimo I* (1565), then continue through Francesco I de' Medici's *studiolo,* kingly apartments and secret passageways before climbing the 95m-tall **Torre di Arnolfo** for exceptional views of the Duomo. Check **Mus.e** (musefirenze.it) for a guided Secret Passages Tour.

The Uffizi

The Uffizi is one of Italy's most visited museums, counting over 4 million tickets sold each year prior to the Covid-19 pandemic. Strolling through its galleries means coming face to face with invaluable works spanning 400 years of history. Giotto, Botticelli, da Vinci, Lippi, Raffaello, Caravaggio and Uccello are just some of the artists found in the galleries originally designed by Giorgio Vasari in 1560 as the administrative offices of Cosimo I's government.

📖 The Pazzi Plot

The most beautiful Renaissance buildings hide much more than precious art collections. Many grim events have marked Florence's history and identity. In 1478 the Pazzi family tried to assassinate Lorenzo Il Magnifico (Lorenzo de' Medici) and his brother Giuliano inside the Duomo. Giuliano was stabbed to death, but Lorenzo survived.

The rotting bodies of the executed conspirators were hung from the windows of Palazzo Vecchio (then Palazzo della Signoria) and Florence's most prominent artists – including Leonardo da Vinci – were commissioned to depict them on the walls of the Bargello Palace (then Palazzo del Podestà), reminding the population of the fate of those planning an insurrection.

■ **Claudia Vannucci,**
Dark Florence tour guide
@theflorenceinsider.com

◎ Uncountable Bees

An equestrian statue of Ferdinando I de' Medici stands in Piazza della Santissima Annunziata. Look closely for the swarm of bees embossed in its base, a symbol of power in 16th-century Florence. Because of their arrangement, the bees are said to be impossible to count from a distance – those who succeed will be rewarded with a stroke of luck.

A section dedicated to previously unseen 16th-century masterpieces opened in 2021, allowing visitors to discover mannerist works of Rosso Fiorentino, Pontormo, Andrea del Sarto and other Late Renaissance greats. Don't miss the **Terrazzo delle Carte Geografiche**, a room dedicated to 16th-century maps that recently reopened after 20 years of renovations.

Palazzo Pitti

The most imposing *palazzo* in the Oltrarno area, commissioned by merchant Luca Pitti in 1446 and purchased by Duchess Eleonora di Toledo, Cosimo I's wife, in 1550, is home to some of Florence's finest museums. These are housed in the apartments that once hosted three of Italy's most powerful dynasties: the Medici (1550–1737), the Habsburg-Lorraine (1739–1860) and the first King of Italy Vittorio Emanuele II (1865–71).

You could spend a whole day exploring the galleries and museums here, but that wouldn't be all. Impressive sights extend well beyond the structure's walls. The piazza, the Giardino di Boboli (p65) and the Palazzo Bianca Cappello are just steps away.

Left Palazzo Vecchio (p45) **Top** Bees on statue of Ferdinando I de' Medici **Above** *Madonna del Cardellino* by Raffaello, Uffizi Gallery

FLORENCE EXPERIENCES

02 LOOKING
for Michelangelo

SCULPTURE | ART | MUSEUMS

Many are the artists who have contributed to making Florence one of the world's top art destinations, but few have left a mark as profound as Michelangelo Buonarroti (1475–1564). Here is how to experience the city through the many expressions of the Renaissance giant.

 How to

Getting around All sights can be reached on foot, but take at least two days to enjoy all of them to the fullest.

When to go Expect queues in the Galleria dell'Accademia, the Cappelle Medicee and the Uffizi (p46). Go early in the morning to avoid crowds, especially in the high season (April and May).

Top tip Michelangelo's monumental tomb, designed by Giorgio Vasari, is found inside the Basilica di Santa Croce; it's open daily until 5.30pm.

TAMASV/SHUTTERSTOCK ©

Michelangelo: The Sculptor

Every Michelangelo-inspired tour should start in the most obvious of places: the artist's family home. **Casa Buonarroti** (Via Ghibellina 70) hosts the *Madonna della Scala* (1491) and the *Battaglia dei Centauri* (1492), two bas-reliefs that Michelangelo completed in his teenage years and which kick-started his career as a Renaissance master. Continue to the **Museo del Bargello** (Via del Proconsolo 4), where a room dedicated to 16th-century Tuscan sculpture houses the exceptional *Bacco* (1497), sculpted during the artist's Roman period, and the unfinished *David-Apollo* (1530).

The outstanding *David* (1501), created from a single marble block when Michelangelo was only 26, awaits in the **Galleria dell'Accademia** (Via Ricasoli 58/60) in all of its 5.17m glory, together with a collection of unfinished figures

THEKLA CLARK/CORBIS VIA GETTY IMAGES ©

◎ **Michelangelo: The Graffiti Artist**

L'Importuno, a rough portrait carved into Palazzo Vecchio's facade, is considered Michelangelo's best-known act of vandalism, allegedly etched with a knife held behind his back. It depicts a Florentine citizen who wouldn't stop bothering the artist when he walked through Piazza della Signoria.

Above left *Tondo Doni* (p51), Uffizi Gallery **Above right** *L'Importuno*, Palazzo Vecchio **Left** *Battaglia dei Centauri*, Casa Buonarroti

trapped in massive white rocks that surround the city's most iconic artwork. Last but not least is the **Museo dell'Opera del Duomo** (Piazza del Duomo 9), where the *Pietà Bandini* (1547–55), one of Michelangelo's last works, sits next to sculptures by Donatello, Arnolfo di Cambio, Ghiberti and Giovanni Pisano.

Michelangelo: The Architect

While the best-known buildings designed by Michelangelo are found in Rome, Florence features two structures within the **Basilica di San Lorenzo** complex that show how the artist's vision developed after he began receiving architectural commissions in the early 16th century. In 1516 Michelangelo was asked by Pope Leone X, son of Lorenzo Il Magnifico, to redesign the basilica's facade. The project never took off, but led to years of architectural experimentation which resulted in the construction of the funerary chapels of the Medici family and the Biblioteca Laurenziana.

The Santo Spirito Crucifix

A little-known work often attributed to Michelangelo is found inside the **Basilica di Santo Spirito**, where the artist lived and studied anatomy in 1492. Deemed lost in the late 18th century, the crucifix was long known to historians only through the writings of Ascanio Condivi and Giorgio Vasari. In 1964 Margrit Lisner, a researcher specialised in 15th-century Tuscan crucifixes, claimed that the sculpture had never actually left its original location – it had only been badly painted over. Although experts still debate Lisner's conclusion, further analysis done in 1999 supported one of the most important art discoveries of the century.

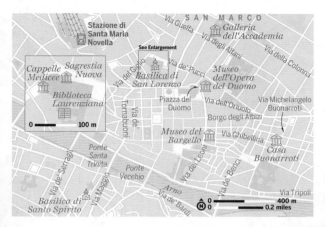

Left Santo Spirito crucifix **Below** Dome of the Sagrestia Nuova, Basilica di San Lorenzo

The wooden model can be seen inside Casa Buonarroti (p49).

The **Sagrestia Nuova** (New Sacristy), an extension of the Basilica di San Lorenzo, was erected between 1520 and 1534 to provide the most prominent members of the Medici family with a regal burial. It is now part of the **Cappelle Medicee museum** where natural light functions as a design element to showcase the symmetrical lines and sculptures of the room throughout the day. Vasari took care of the final touches after 1556, when Michelangelo had moved permanently to Rome.

The **Biblioteca Laurenziana**, also found in the Basilica di San Lorenzo, was designed to hold the vast text collection of Cosimo the Elder which was later added to by Lorenzo il Magnifico; behind Michelangelo's elegant vestibule you can still find 11,000 manuscripts, 1681 original 16th-century books, and the largest collection of Egyptian papyri in Italy.

Michelangelo: The Painter

Only one panel painting completed by Michelangelo has survived to this day – the *Tondo Doni* (1505–06), a circular tempera representation of the Holy Family visible in Room 35 of the Uffizi (p46) in its original frame (attributed to Michelangelo himself).

03 More than the **DUOMO**

ARCHITECTURE | ART | RELIGION

Florence's most iconic building is a spectacle that never ceases to amaze, but the Cattedrale di Santa Maria del Fiore is only one of the many treasures nestled in Piazza del Duomo. Art, architecture and exceptional views all await.

🗺 How to

Accessing Santa Maria del Fiore Entry to the ground floor of the church is free. Remember to cover your legs and shoulders or you won't be let in.

Tickets Choose between the all-access Brunelleschi Pass (€30); the Giotto Pass (€20), which includes entrance to all sites apart from the dome; or the limited Ghiberti Pass (€15). All are valid for 72 hours and can be purchase at duomo. firenze.it.

Well-earned views Climbing the dome and the campanile is no joke – be prepared to climb 463 and 414 steps, respectively.

The Cathedral

When the project came to completion in 1436, the **Cattedrale di Santa Maria del Fiore** (also known as Florence Cathedral) was the largest church ever constructed. Many great minds applied their vision during the 140 years it took to build – from Arnolfo di Cambio to Filippo Brunelleschi, represented in statues on its southern side – and, in the end, erected a structure that would become an architectural achievement like no other. Enter to admire Giorgio Vasari's and Federico Zuccari's *Last Judgment* (1572–79) adorning the interior of Brunelleschi's dome, then climb the cupola for one of the best views of the city's red rooftops.

The Campanile

For more unforgettable views (and possible knee pain), walk up the sky-scraping

🔭 Best Views

Piazzale Michelangelo The best-known spot to see the city from above.

Orti del Parnaso Little-known park in the city's north for a view without a crowd.

Fiesole A hillside town with incredible views from the Convento di San Francesco.

Above left Cattedrale di Santa Maria del Fiore **Above right** Museo dell'Opera del Duomo (p55) **Left** Doorway of the Battistero di San Giovanni (p54)

Campanile di Giotto, a testament to the Gothic style loved by leaders and artists during the Renaissance. Using white, green and red marble to reflect the exterior of the Duomo, Giotto began building the 84.7m-tall bell tower in 1334, but died three years later, leaving the project in the hands of Andrea Pisano and Francesco Talenti. The narrow staircase leads to the panoramic platform that Talenti added in 1359 to seal off the tower – get there for unmatched views of the Duomo and the city.

Battistero di San Giovanni

Built on the remains of a baptistery dating back to the 5th century CE, the octagonal-shaped Battistero di San Giovanni is one of the oldest churches in the city and a key example of the dichromatic Florentine Romanesque architectural style that developed between the 11th and 13th centuries. Inside you'll find a series of marvellous mosaics designed by Cimabue, Coppo di Marcovaldo, Meliore and other 13th-century greats who drew inspiration from

Florence's Other Churches

Santa Croce This 12,000-sq-metre Gothic masterpiece contains the tombs of Michelangelo, astronomer Galileo Galilei and writer Foscolo.

Santa Maria Novella By the train station, home to the prodigious Filippo Strozzi Chapel painted by Filippo Lippi in 1502.

San Miniato al Monte Set in one of the highest locations in the city, this Romanesque church dates back to the 11th century CE.

Santa Maria del Carmine Home of the Brancacci Chapel, frescoed during the early 15th century by Masaccio and Masolino da Panicale.

Orsanmichele Built in the 14th century as a grain marketplace, this unusual church is surrounded by 14 statues featuring the patron saints of the once-powerful craft guilds.

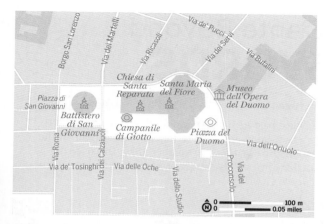

Left San Miniato al Monte
Below Mosaics, Battistero
di San Giovanni

Byzantine art, telling biblical myths in concentric circles on a golden background. Before 1990, three monumental doors designed by Andrea Pisano and Lorenzo Ghiberti gave access to the baptistery – what you see today are copies, with the originals recently placed in the Museo dell'Opera del Duomo after nearly a decade of restoration.

Florentine Sculpture

The **Museo dell'Opera del Duomo** contains one of the largest collections of Florentine sculpture in the world, with 750 pieces spread across 28 rooms, including Arnolfo di Cambio's *Madonna della Natività e Angeli* (1296–1300) and Donatello's *Maddalena Penitente* (1453–55). Pisano's *Porta Sud* (1330–36), which depicts the story of Florence's patron saint John the Baptist, and Ghiberti's *Porta Nord* (1403–24) and *Porta del Paradiso* (1425–52) are also essential stops to see Florentine sculpture.

Chiesa di Santa Reparata

The cathedral's right nave gives access to the remains of the ancient Chiesa di Santa Reparata, the foundation of Santa Maria del Fiore believed to have been built to celebrate the victory of the Roman and Florentine army over the Ostrogoths in 405 or 406 CE. It was only in the late 1960s that archaeologists rediscovered the structure and were able to trace its evolution.

04 Dante Beyond WORDS

LITERATURE | HISTORY | CULTURE

▬▬▬ Over seven centuries have passed since Dante Alighieri's death in 1321, but vivid traces of Florence's best-known man of letters are still visible on the city's streets and continue to inspire writers and visitors alike. Discover the stories that have made Florence one of Italy's most prestigious literary centres, built on the legacy of the *Divine Comedy*.

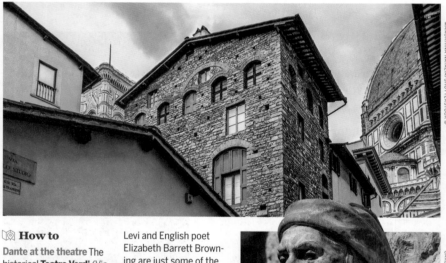

MANOKHINA NATALIA/SHUTTERSTOCK ©

🗺 How to

Dante at the theatre The historical **Teatro Verdi** (Via Ghibellina 99) occasionally brings the *Divine Comedy* onto the stage and it's a show worth seeing. Check the program at teatroverdifirenze.it.

More than Dante Russian author Fyodor Dostoevsky, Italian writer Carlo Levi and English poet Elizabeth Barrett Browning are just some of the legendary writers who have found inspiration in Florence. Look for marble plaques with their names around Piazza Pitti.

Did you know? Dante is considered the father of the Italian language.

CARL DEABREU PHOTOGRAPHY/SHUTTERSTOCK ©

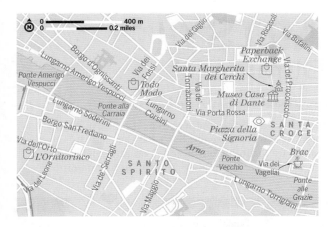

Top left Museo Casa di Dante
Bottom left Bust of Dante Alighieri
by Augusto Rivalta

Dante's origins Many of the city's most photographed landmarks didn't exist in the Florence of the Middle Ages, when rich families ruled and fought from their *case torri* (tower houses), such as Torre de' Barbadori on Borgo San Jacopo or Torre de' Cerchi on Via dei Cerchi. The **Museo Casa di Dante** (Via Santa Margherita 1), located steps away from Piazza della Signoria and the Badia Fiorentina monastery, will bring you back to that era through historical documents, everyday utensils and clothing worn at the time. Despite its name, the museum is not the place where Dante grew up after being baptised in the Battistero di San Giovanni (p54) in 1265; but it is still one of the best-preserved corners of medieval Florence, employed since 1965 to tribute the great poet and writer.

Santa Margherita dei Cerchi Legend has it that here, in Via Santa Margherita, Dante first met Beatrice Portinari, the woman who scholars believe inspired one of the *Divine Comedy's* leading characters and shaped the epic poem to become one of the world's greatest pieces of literature. Married to Simone de' Bardi, Beatrice died at the age of 24 in 1290, causing Dante to fall into a deep crisis which would affect his later work. Inside the church, a plaque indicates Beatrice's tomb (although it is likely that her remains are actually buried in Santa Croce, with her husband's body); here heartbroken visitors leave notes hoping for Dante's muse to help fix romantic troubles.

📖 Independent Bookshops

Paperback Exchange Your go-to destination for English-language books in the heart of the city.

Todo Modo Walk through the wooden bookshelves and find yourself in a hidden cafe where literature is served with a side of natural wine. Hungry? Order the *testaroli*.

L'Ornitorinco A literary oasis on San Frediano's Via di Camaldoli. Enjoy an espresso surrounded by graphic novels, indie magazines and books carefully selected by welcoming Lilith.

Brac Designer interiors that make you want to sit down and catch up with that maximalist novel you've promised you'll finish someday.

05 ARTSY
Oltrarno

CONTEMPORARY ART | FOOD & DRINK | NEIGHBOURHOOD WALK

▬▬▬ The Oltrarno neighbourhoods on the southern side of the Arno might not boast as many landmarks as central Florence, but what they lack in famous monuments they make up for in unconventional galleries, delicious food and live music venues. Get your creative juices flowing in Santo Spirito and San Frediano.

HEMIS/ALAMY STOCK PHOTO ©

🏃 In Pratolini's Footsteps

San Frediano before gentrification is hard to imagine, but reading Nobel Prize nominee Vasco Pratolini is perhaps the best way to get a sense of the neighbourhood's working-class roots. Walking through Piazza del Cestello, Piazza Tasso and Via della Chiesa with the right book in hand is often enough to experience the city from a different perspective.

🗺 Trip Notes

Getting around Cross either Ponte Vecchio or Ponte Santa Trinità and explore Oltrarno on foot.

Sleeping soundly This side of the Arno can be a great base for exploring Florence, but know that Piazza Santo Spirito and Borgo San Frediano get loud during summer evenings, as bar crowds spill onto the streets.

Family fun The bookshop **Todo Modo Dilà** (Via dei Serragli 18) runs chess workshops for kids of all ages every Saturday.

■ Recommended by Giulia Cosentino & Vittoria Maschietto, *literary tour guides*
@leragazzedisanfrediano

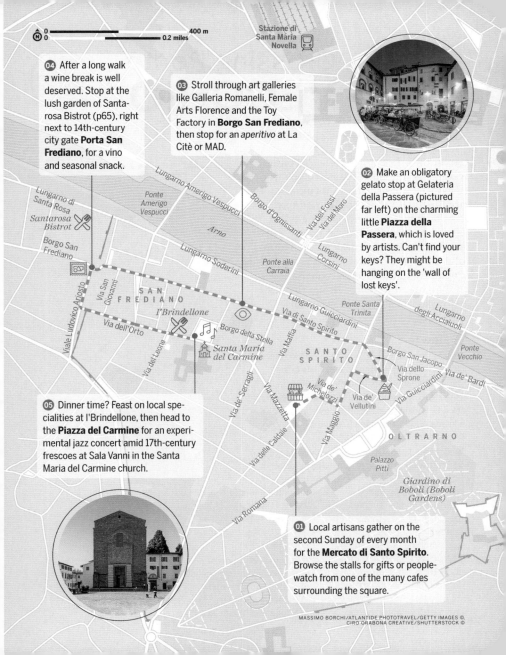

04 After a long walk a wine break is well deserved. Stop at the lush garden of Santarosa Bistrot (p65), right next to 14th-century city gate **Porta San Frediano**, for a vino and seasonal snack.

03 Stroll through art galleries like Galleria Romanelli, Female Arts Florence and the Toy Factory in **Borgo San Frediano**, then stop for an *aperitivo* at La Cité or MAD.

02 Make an obligatory gelato stop at Gelateria della Passera (pictured far left) on the charming little **Piazza della Passera**, which is loved by artists. Can't find your keys? They might be hanging on the 'wall of lost keys'.

05 Dinner time? Feast on local specialities at l'Brindellone, then head to the **Piazza del Carmine** for an experimental jazz concert amid 17th-century frescoes at Sala Vanni in the Santa Maria del Carmine church.

01 Local artisans gather on the second Sunday of every month for the **Mercato di Santo Spirito**. Browse the stalls for gifts or people-watch from one of the many cafes surrounding the square.

0 400 m
0 0.2 miles

Stazione di Santa Maria Novella

Lungarno di Santa Rosa
Santarosa Bistrot
Borgo San Frediano
Ponte Amerigo Vespucci
Lungarno Amerigo Vespucci
Borgo d'Ognissanti
Via dei Fossi
Via del Moro
Arno
Lungarno Soderini
Ponte alla Carraia
Lungarno Corsini
Viale Ludovico Ariosto
Via San Giovanni
SAN FREDIANO
l'Brindellone
Via dell'Orto
Via del Leone
Borgo della Stella
Santa Maria del Carmine
Lungarno Guicciardini
Ponte Santa Trinita
Lungarno degli Acciaiuoli
Via Maffia
Lungarno di Santo Spirito
SANTO SPIRITO
Borgo San Jacopo
Ponte Vecchio
Via dello Sprone
Via Guicciardini
Via de' Bardi
Via de' Serragli
Via Mazzetta
Via de' Michelozzi
Via de' Vellutini
Via delle Caldaie
Via Maggio
OLTRARNO
Palazzo Pitti
Via Romana
Giardino di Boboli (Boboli Gardens)

06 Crossing Ponte **VECCHIO**

ARCHITECTURE | CRAFTS | PHOTOGRAPHY

Built in 1345, Florence's Ponte Vecchio is one of the city's best-known symbols, both because of its unusual architecture and its convoluted past. Layers of history connect the city on opposite sides of the Arno river – walk across cobblestones under the shadow of the Corridoio Vasariano (Vasari Corridor), amid silverware artisans and high-end jewellers in the romantic yet mysterious atmosphere of this Renaissance icon.

🗺 How to

Getting around The bridge can get crowded during the day. Visit early in the morning or late in the evening to enjoy a more relaxed experience.

Arno cruising Check out the Ponte Vecchio from below by booking a cruise on a *barchetto* (small traditional boat). **I Renaioli** (renaioli.it) runs hour-long boat trips from May to October.

Sunset shot Jump over to Ponte Santa Trinita at sunset time to watch the bridge turn red as the day ends.

The medieval bridge The 48 uneven shops perched above the bridge's three stone arches have survived both the Nazi bombing of 1944 and the destructive flood that hit the city in 1966. Stroll through the *lungarni* (the two streets that run parallel to the river) for a perfect shot of the bridge

then catch a live performance by street musician Claudio Spadi, who plays most evenings by the monument to Benvenuto Cellini.

Bling bling As you cross Ponte Vecchio you'll quickly notice that every shop here is a jewellery store. Originally, the bridge was mostly pop-

Top right Ponte Vecchio
Bottom right Jewellery shop, Ponte Vecchio

BOTOND HORVATH/SHUTTERSTOCK ©

💐 Light Festival

During the **F-Light Festival** (flightfirenze.it) from December to early January, the city's favourite bridge and many other iconic buildings – including the Basilica di San Lorenzo – turn into canvases for grand art installations projected on their walls.

ulated by *beccai* (butchers), but in 1593 Grand Duke Ferdinando I, who could not stand the smell of meat and the insalubrious state of the market, evicted all businesses involved in 'vile arts', allowing only goldsmiths and jewellers to trade on the bridge. Just a few local artisans continue to operate on Ponte Vecchio, but the Museo degli Argenti inside nearby Palazzo Pitti (p47) pays testimony to the Florentine goldsmith tradition.

Corridoio Vasariano The passageway designed by Giorgio Vasari in 1565 that connects Palazzo Pitti with Palazzo Vecchio still runs across Ponte Vecchio's eastern edge. Cosimo I commissioned this 760m-long tunnel to allow for safe crossing between the Medici's new residence and the governmental offices. At time of research, the tunnel was due to reopen to the public in late 2022. Keep an eye on uffizi.it/en/corridoio-vasariano for updates.

CHRISTIAN MUELLER/GETTY IMAGES ©

ANTONIO MASIELLO/GETTY IMAGES ©

A Game of Violence

FOUR TEAMS, ONE BALL, MUCH BLOOD

Combining elements of football, boxing and rugby, *calcio storico fiorentino* is not a sport for the faint-hearted. Each year in June, a temporary sand arena set up in Piazza Santa Croce turns historic rivalries into a blood-soaked tournament of one of the world's most vicious sports.

Each year, as spring turns into summer, Florentine doctors and nurses prepare for one of the most awaited events of the year. Standing near the five ambulances parked around Piazza Santa Croce, the city's medical staff listens to the crowd of 4000 cheering for 54 men in traditional costumes running on the *sabbione* – a 100m by 50m sand arena set up for the occasion – in the attempt to score a point by any means available. Kicks, bare-knuckle punches, clashes and tackles – no strategy is off limits during the yearly *calcio storico* tournament, the sporting event dating back to the 16th century, held in June since 1930.

Recent history shows that 'incidents' are to be expected – in 2019, 44-year-old Bianchi player Fabrizio Valleri was rushed to the hospital due to the fracture of several ribs and the puncture of a lung, while in 2017, dozens of police in riot gear entered the field to stop the brawls happening after Azzurri players were dismissed for hitting three referees in the face. That's not it. In 2005 the game was suspended after beatings turned the match into a full-scale mass fight – with 43 of 54 players legally prosecuted for excessive violence – and in 2001, seven players from opposing teams had to be transported to separate hospitals due to chest contusions and excoriations.

Despite the rough nature of the game, the three matches that form the competition – two semifinals and a final held on 24 June, the day Florence celebrates its patron saint John the Baptist – remain fixed on Florence's calendar and folklore. Four teams, or 'colours', representing the historical neighbourhoods of the city – Santa Maria Novella's Rossi (Reds), Santa Croce's Azzurri (Blues),

Above left and right *Calcio storico* players **Middle** Parade during *calcio storico* contest, Piazza Santa Croce

Santo Spirito's Bianchi (Whites) and San Giovanni's Verdi (Greens) – compete to score the highest amount of *cacce* (hunts) by carrying the ball into the opponent's net at the end of the field, combining elements of rugby, boxing and football. All the *calcianti* (players) have to be either born in Florence or be city residents for at least 10 years. Games last 50 minutes and are played in temperatures that often reach 30°C. Substitutions are not allowed.

The origins of *calcio storico* are unclear, but 1530 is usually referred to as the year when the sport became institutionalised. At the time, football was already widely practised in the streets of Florence, with official games organised by local governments during Carnival. When the imperial troops of Charles V, an ally of the Medici family who wanted to reestablish control over the city, threatened to attack the city, the Florentines decided to play the football games they had planned anyway to prove their fearlessness to the enemy. The Bianchi and the Verdi played against each while the city was under fire on 17 February and the *partita dell'assedio* (the game of the siege) became an enduring symbol of resistance. The *calcio storico* that is played today is a reenactment of that legendary match and glory is the only prize to be earned from spilt blood, since none of the *calcianti* is paid to enter the brutal *sabbione*.

> **Kicks, bare-knuckle punches, clashes and tackles – no strategy is off limits during the yearly tournament.**

07 Botanical
ESCAPES

GARDENS | WALKS | VIEWS

■■■ Take a break from markets, museums and cathedrals to immerse yourself in one of the many green spaces dotting the city. Explore carefully planned landscapes designed for the powerful courts of the past or leave tourist trails behind for a blissful break in a hidden oasis.

DAN74/SHUTTERSTOCK ©

🗺️ How to

When to go City gardens are open year-round, but spring is the best season to visit as this is when the city's flora comes to life.

More than flowers Download the free Botanical Map by **Unusual Florence** (unusual florence.blogspot.com)

to discover the city's century-old trees.

Plant shopping The **Tuscan Horticultural Society** (societa toscanaorticultura.it) organises one of the city's most picturesque flower markets in the Giardino dell'Orticoltura during the last week of April.

TOM IRACI/SHUTTERSTOCK ©

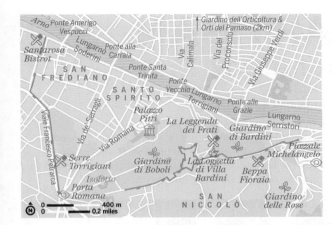

Top left Wisteria passageway, Giardino Bardini **Bottom left** Tepidarium, Giardino dell'Orticoltura

Florence's most famous city garden The **Giardino di Boboli** dates back to the Medici era and covers over 45 hectares, extending from Palazzo Pitti. Monumental fountains and sculptures dot the green expanse that inspired the European court garden tradition. Enter at Porta Romana, walk by the majestic Fontana dell'Oceano and continue up to Forte di Belvedere for unbeatable views.

Spring blooms Hidden under Piazzale Michelangelo in Viale Giuseppe Poggi, **Giardino delle Rose**, Florence's rose garden, is best experienced in late spring, when the 350 species of flowers carefully grown here are in full bloom. A permanent exhibition of 12 sculptures by Belgian architect Jean-Michel Folon (1934–2005) can also be seen here. Another spring favourite is the terraced garden surrounding Villa Bardini, **Giardino Bardini**. Climb up the baroque staircase to reach the wisteria passageway, where you can admire Florence from behind a bright violet frame between April and May. Stop at **La Loggetta di Villa Bardini** for a thirst-quenching *aperitivo* overlooking the Duomo.

A quiet retreat A lesser-known park in the northern part of the city, **Giardino dell'Orticoltura** offers a space to chill away from the crowds extending from a 19th-century tepidarium. Stay for a picnic or walk up to the adjacent **Orti del Parnaso** where a massive sculpture of a snake crawling down the staircase leads to an unspoiled city view.

🍽 Garden Bars & Restaurants

Beppa Fioraia Take a seat in this idyllic spot between the Giardino Bardini and the Giardino delle Rose to snack on a *tagliere* (tasting platter) covered in local cheeses and cured meats.

Serre Torrigiani Located in the elegant Giardino Torrigiani, this seasonal bistro is one of Florence's best hidden treasures.

Santarosa Bistrot Chill on one of the loungers in the park as you sip an *aperitivo* in this lush corner of San Frediano.

La Leggenda dei Frati Enjoy an unforgettable dinner at this Michelin-starred restaurant on the edge of the Giardino Bardini.

08 ARTISAN
for a Day

ARTISANS | COURSES | CRAFTS

Since the days when the Medici family commissioned sumptuous handmade furnishings for the south-of-the-Arno Pitti Palace, the Oltrarno district has been ground zero for Florence's woodworkers, bookbinders, jewellers and paper-marbling mavens. While the bulk of artisanal activity is still concentrated in that area, new talents are carrying on old traditions all over the city.

ARNO IMAGES/GETTY IMAGES ©

🗺 How to

Book ahead Committed artisans have client orders to fill before they can entertain visitors. Don't show up unannounced to a workspace and ask for a demo or a lesson – unless you're ready to commit to a real apprenticeship! Ask about availability in advance.

Dress the part Florentine craftspeople have no room to be fussy. Follow suit! Before dabbling in any artisan activity, pull your hair back, remove earrings and jewellery, and wear comfortable clothing that won't easily snag.

ATLANTIDE PHOTOTRAVEL/GETTY IMAGES ©

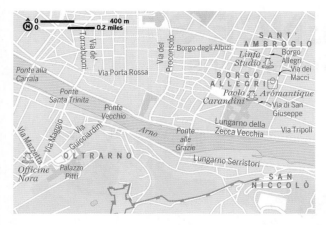

Top left Jeweller, Florence
Bottom left Parchment leaf made by Paolo Carandini

Open to visitors Many of the up-and-coming *maestri* (masters) of Florentine artisanship are as committed to tradition as their purist predecessors – but also embrace the changing world a bit more readily. A growing number of artisans – from goldsmiths to ceramicists to perfumers – have recognised the value of education in building awareness and preserving their practices. Curious dilettantes and travellers are increasingly being welcomed to workbenches for lessons and activities.

A serious workshop The collective **Officine Nora** (Via dei Preti 2-4r; officinenora.it) was one of the pioneers of this more participatory approach to Florentine artisanship. A shared workspace for Italian and international jewellery makers – all with a dizzying variety of styles – it's spearheaded by progressive Florentine Margherita de Martino Norante. Don't call Officine Nora a shop, nor a school – it's a bona-fide *bottega* (workspace), but with some contemporary, visitor-friendly twists: visitors can arrange tailor-made souvenir workshops or jeweller-for-a-day experiences with one of the regulars.

Borgo Allegri crafts and courses On the opposite side of the river, beyond the hordes of Santa Croce, the Sant'Ambrogio neighbourhood is growing in its craft credibility. The hidden **Borgo Allegri**, in particular, is becoming a hotbed of makers. It's home to **Paolo Carandini** (Borgo Allegri 7r; paolocarandini.net), who uses parchment and dyed calfskin to fashion cheeky, often cinematically themed cigar boxes and containers, as well as **Linfa Studio** (Borgo Allegri 60r; linfa studiogallery.com), where jewellers Valentina and Francesca offer private and group filigree courses.

⚗️ Secret Scents

Perfumery has been part of the Florentine fabric since the Dominican monks of Santa Maria Novella began growing medicinal herbs for all manner of ailments. Architect turned aromatherapist Maria Letizia Longo is a dedicated and passionate perfumer who carries on the centuries-old practice, creating home diffusers, perfumes, scented bookmarks and essential oils. Her laboratory **Arômantique** (aromantique. it) is headquartered in Sant'Ambrogio, but you won't stumble on it (nor its secret garden, nor Longo's addictive hands-on workshops) without writing to her first.

FLORENCE'S
Culinary Inventions

01 Lampredotto
A street food classic made with a section of the cow's stomach cooked in vegetable broth, covered in green sauce and served in a round sandwich. Try it at Il Trippaio di San Frediano, or opt for the vegan version invented by elusive chef Gaetano Cerasuolo.

02 Schiacciata
A flat, focaccia-like bread baked in the oven and seasoned with extra virgin olive oil and a hefty amount of salt. No need to stand in line for hours at All'Antico Vinaio – enjoy it on its own at Forno Pugi or filled with local cheeses and meats at Sapori Toscani.

03 Negroni
Created by Count Camillo Negroni in 1919 by substituting soda water with gin in an Americano cocktail he deemed too light. This Florentine classic will get you going through the night (hangover warning). Try it at Caffè Rivoire.

04 Cantucci
The Medici were already enjoying these dry biscuits often filled with almonds in the 16th century. Best when dipped in Vin Santo (dessert wine), get some at Il Cantuccio di San Lorenzo.

05 Gelato Buontalenti
Renaissance artist Bernardo Buontalenti is said to have invented gelato in the 16th century. So why not try the flavour that takes his name – made with cream, sugar and eggs – at Gelateria Badiani?

06 Schiacciata all'uva
The sweet version of the *schiacciata,* made with juicy red grapes. Eat a delicious slice after the grape harvest in September at Forno Becagli.

07 Pappa al pomodoro
A 'poor' dish of the Tuscan tradition that is as tasty as it is simple. It's made by cooking stale bread with tomatoes, garlic, basil and the ever-present olive oil. Order a plate at Osteria Santo Spirito.

Listings

BEST OF THE REST

Even More Museums...

Museo Galileo

Located near the Uffizi gallery, this museum showcases over 1000 documents and scientific instruments, including those used by astronomer Galileo Galilei, who lived nearby in Costa S Giorgio.

Museo Novecento

One of Florence's newest museums, located in the rooms of a former hospital in Piazza Santa Maria Novella, features an intriguing selection of 20th-century Italian art.

Gucci Garden

A glimpse into the history of the fashion powerhouse through a collection of iconic pieces that have made the history of the brand, from handbags and luggage to clothing and accessories.

Museo Marino Marini

The largest collection of works by the famed 20th-century Pistoiese artist is hosted in a hidden square in the former church of San Pancrazio.

Casa Martelli

The palace where one of Florence's most influential families lived from the 16th to the 20th century opens to the public every Saturday morning. Guided tours are free, but only in Italian.

Palazzo Strozzi

One of the city's best known Renaissance palaces hosts a rotating program of contemporary art exhibitions. Past shows have included Jeff Koons, Natalia Goncharova and Marina Abramovich. Check out the program at palazzostrozzi.org.

Museo Stibbert

Located on the Montughi hill, this museum features an eclectic mix of art, weapons and armour collected during the 19th century by British entrepreneur Frederick Stibbert (1838–1906).

Holy Landmarks & Architecture

Basilica di San Marco

In the homonymous piazza, this lesser-known church contains a series of chapels designed by Flemish artist Giambologna, dating back to the late 16th century.

Basilica della Santissima Annunziata

The city's main Marian church, dating back to the 13th century, has hosted many great Florentine artists over the centuries, including Pontormo, Rosso Fiorentino and Andrea del Sarto whose mannerist paintings can be admired in the beautiful Chiostrino dei Votivi.

Chiesa di Ognissanti

Inside this little church in Borgo Ognissanti you'll find Sandro Botticelli's tombstone. In 1480 the author of *The Birth of Venus* worked here with painter Domenico Ghirlandaio.

Museo Galileo

ATLANTIDE PHOTOTRAVEL/GETTY IMAGES ©

Cimitero degli Inglesi

The resting place of many famous authors, including Elizabeth Barrett Browning and Walter Savage Landor, the English Cemetery is an expansive, awe-inspiring burial ground open since 1827 and featuring hundreds of intricately carved marble headstones.

 Creative Crafts & Old-School Finds

Farmacia di Santa Maria Novella

With over 800 years of continuous activity, the Santa Maria Novella Pharmacy is considered to be the oldest apothecary in the world, still selling mysterious potions manufactured following old-fashioned methods.

Manifattura Tabacchi

Pop-up shops, events spaces, co-working areas and more in this redeveloped industrial complex near the Cascine park. Check what's on at manifatturatabacchi.com.

Bartolucci

A woodwork workshop specialising in artisanal, one-of-a-kind toys and Pinocchio-inspired souvenirs located in Via della Condotta. Bring your kids for some analog fun.

Aquaflor

An inviting scent leads to this perfume lab in Borgo Santa Croce, which offers a wide selection of bespoke fragrances, soaps, candles and make-your-own perfume experiences in an elegant, old-charm showroom.

Alessandro Dari Gioielli

Enter the magical atmosphere of this dimly lit museum-slash-workshop in San Niccolò, where master goldsmith Alessandro Dari creates wearable works of art.

GABRIEL BOUYS/AFP VIA GETTY IMAGES ©

Farmacia di Santa Maria Novella

Coffee Breaks

Ditta Artigianale

Your go-to destination for speciality coffee in Florence. With four locations open around the city centre, serving selected beans in an international atmosphere, you are never too far from a perfectly brewed caffeine kick.

Caffè Gilli

Running since 1773, one of the oldest cafes in Florence serves excellent espresso in an art nouveau atmosphere that will take you back in time a couple of centuries.

Caffè Lietta

Delicious pastries to pair with your cappuccino in this welcoming space near Piazza della Libertà. Stop for a *pistacchio* croissant for a sweet breakfast before heading to the sights in the city centre.

Brunch, Lunch & Street Food

I Due Fratellini   €

An institution of the Florentine street food scene, the 'little brothers' serve dozens of different sandwiches filled with local delicacies from their hole-in-the-wall shop in Via dei Cimatori. Expect lunchtime queues.

Trattoria Guelfa €

This local favourite just steps from the Mercato Centrale serves a complete Tuscan lunch for €13. Choose your first and second course from the hand-written, daily-changing menu.

Semel €

A traditional street *paninoteca* (sandwich bar) in the Sant'Ambrogio neighbourhood, serving freshly made sandwiches filled with creative combinations of cured meats, fish, cheeses and sauces accompanied by a healthy dose of wine.

Il Budellino €

Nothing is more traditional than a bowl of tripe in tomato sauce served next to a glass of Sangiovese. Take a seat inside or people-watch while eating directly on Via dei Neri.

Amblé €€

Steps away from Ponte Vecchio, Amblé cares about the quality of its food as much as for the cafe's design. The good news? Every piece of furniture you see is available for purchase.

Raw €€

As the name suggests, Santo Spirito's Raw specialises in (mostly) uncooked dishes made with vegan, organic ingredients. Try a raw pizza and follow up with a raw cacao cake.

Melaleuca €€

Freshly made cinnamon rolls straight out of the oven are one of the menu highlights of Santa Croce's favourite brunch cafe.

Le Vespe €€

Seasonally inspired vegan- and vegetarian-friendly food with an international touch served daily in this Via Ghibellina brunch spot run by a Florentine-Canadian team.

La Ménagère €€

The theatrical decor attracts those willing to splurge for an Instagram-friendly meal, but expect tasty flavour combinations and a great cocktail list too.

⚔ Experimental & Refined Dining

Osteria dei Centopoveri €

A busy, affordable, locally loved *osteria* nestled in a back alley close to Piazza Santa Maria Novella. The wide selection of dishes ranges from Tuscan meats to pizza.

Trattoria Tredici Gobbi €€

You can't really go wrong with this historic little trattoria in Via del Porcellana proudly preserving its old-school rustic vibe. Try a generous portion of *rigatoni*.

Cuculia €€

A colourful, experimental menu with many vegan and vegetarian options prepared with hyperlocal ingredients served in an intimate space in Via dei Serragli.

Guné €€

No detail goes unchecked in this San Frediano restaurant, whose menu revisits Tuscan tradition through Basilicata-influenced flavours.

Konnubio €€€

Reinventing Italian classics is what Konnubio does best. Expect the unexpected when choosing dishes such as the risotto with chocolate or the purple noodles.

La Ménagère

La Giostra €€€

Brick arches, white tablecloths, a plethora of candles and rustic decor create the perfect ambience to enjoy refined Tuscan cuisine. You'll think the food menu is extensive until you've seen the wine list.

Enoteca Pinchiorri €€€

One of the city's great dining destinations and the only Florentine restaurant boasting three Michelin stars. Located in an 18th-century palace in Via Ghibellina, the kitchen run by French chef Annie Féolde creates inimitable culinary experiences.

Enoteca Pinchiorri

Beer, Wine & Cocktails

Mostodolce

A wide selection of craft beers at a fair price in a relaxed pub atmosphere on Via Nazionale. Try the Belgian-style house ale Martellina.

Il Santino

The massive list of top-quality wines attracts way too many drinkers for the handful of tables available in this cosy *enoteca*. Get your *calice* and mingle with the locals spilling onto Via Santo Spirito.

Manifattura

You won't be able to order a margarita in this quirky cocktail bar focused on Italian spirits. But don't despair – the friendly staff will recommend a valid alternative, starting from the huge selection of *amari* (bitter liqueurs).

Bulli & Balene

If you thought a *spritz* could only be made with Aperol, Bulli & Balene is here to change your mind. Take a seat looking out onto the charming Piazza della Passera and choose some *cicchetti* (Venetian tapas) to go with your cocktail.

Babae

Located in Santo Spirito, Babae has one of the last functioning wine windows in the city. Head to the window and ring the leaf-shaped bell to order your preferred vino, which will be handed out through the aperture.

Locale

Named among the 100 best bars in the world, Locale attracts a stylish crowd thanks to its beautiful vertical garden wall and one-of-a-kind seasonal craft cocktail list.

Il Piccolo

Intimate atmosphere, unique decor and great pre- or post-dinner cocktails served in this LGBTIQ-friendly venue hidden behind Piazza Santa Croce.

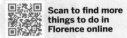

Scan to find more things to do in Florence online

SIENA & CENTRAL TUSCANY

MEDIEVAL TOWNS | TRADITIONS | CONTEMPORARY ART

Experience Siena & Central Tuscany online

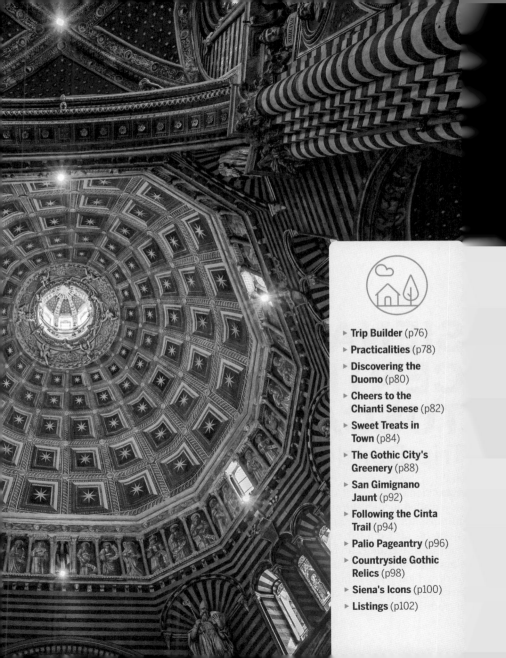

Day-trip to medieval Manhattan and avant-garde art hub **San Gimignano** (p92)

🚌 *1hr from Siena*

○ Pancole

● Il Castagano

Colle di
Val d'Elsa ○

● **Volterra**

Be dazzled by Siena's stunning **Cattedrale di Santa Maria Assunta** and the impressive Piccolomini Library inside (p80)

🚶 *3mins from Piazza del Campo*

SIENA & CENTRAL TUSCANY
Trip Builder

Siena is the stuff Tuscan fairy tales are made of: a walled medieval town spread across three hilltops. But while life in the area is leisurely and sweet, it's far from frozen in time: sure, centuries-old traditions like the Palio horse race play on, but equally prominent are the innovative winemakers at work, art gallerists bringing a modern edge to magical old towns, and chefs playing with the tenets of traditional cuisine.

Explore the many layers of legends at the awe-inspiring **Abbazia di San Galgano**, the abbey without a roof (p98)

🚗 *40mins from Siena*

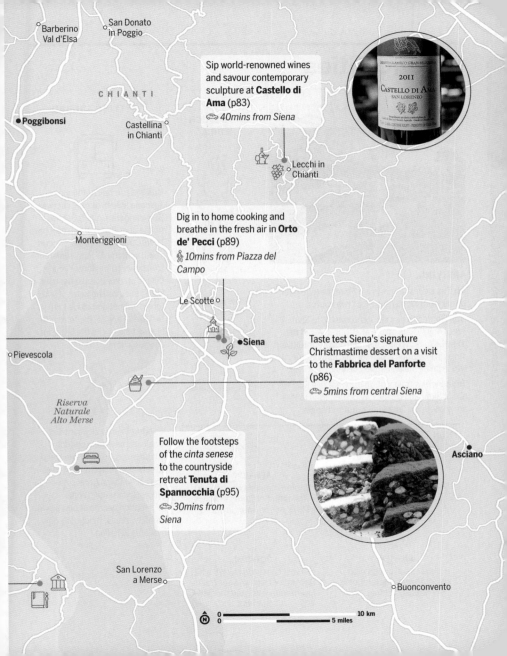

Sip world-renowned wines and savour contemporary sculpture at **Castello di Ama** (p83)
🚗 *40mins from Siena*

Dig in to home cooking and breathe in the fresh air in **Orto de' Pecci** (p89)
🚶 *10mins from Piazza del Campo*

Taste test Siena's signature Christmastime dessert on a visit to the **Fabbrica del Panforte** (p86)
🚗 *5mins from central Siena*

Follow the footsteps of the *cinta senese* to the countryside retreat **Tenuta di Spannocchia** (p95)
🚗 *30mins from Siena*

Barberino Val d'Elsa

San Donato in Poggio

CHIANTI

Poggibonsi

Castellina in Chianti

Lecchi in Chianti

Monteriggioni

Le Scotte

Siena

Pievescola

Riserva Naturale Alto Merse

Asciano

San Lorenzo a Merse

Buonconvento

0   10 km
0   5 miles

Practicalities

SERGIO DI PASQUALE LUCI/GETTY IMAGES ©

ARRIVING

Air The closest airports are Florence (one hour by car from Siena) and Pisa (two hours).

Bus Florence's bus station connects to Siena-Via Tozzi; buy tickets online at at-bus.it. Avoid the 'Diretta' (direct) option, which counterintuitively stops in Poggibonsi. Opt for the 'Rapida' line, which takes the *autostrada* instead.

Train Siena's train station is in Piazzale Rosselli, about 3km outside the city centre; train routes are sometimes limited or require changes.

HOW MUCH FOR A

Cappuccino
€1.30

Glass of Chianti
Classico €6

Trattoria dinner
€30

GETTING AROUND

Bus You can buy Autolinee Toscane tickets to move between Siena and the Chianti Senese online at at-bus.it. If you purchase tickets from a shop, bar or newsstand with the AT logo, remember to validate (timestamp) your tickets on board at the designated kiosk; fines can be heavy if you forget. Tabnet and Moovit are two useful apps – the former for buying tickets and the latter for checking times.

Walking Siena's city centre is small and navigable on foot, but be prepared for some steep streets and sharp turns. A free app called Siena Accessible (accessibile.siena.it) offers information geared at people with mobility issues, though it's only available in Italian.

WHEN TO GO

JAN–MAR
Siena quietens down after 6 January; March brings the Sienese New Year.

APR–JUN
Unpredictable April showers; mild temperatures in May. More visitors later in spring.

JUL–SEP
Palio season brings high temperatures. September is less scorching.

OCT–DEC
Harvest season is always a hit. December brings sweet treats, kid-friendly fairs and medieval markets.

EATING & DRINKING

Cucina povera (peasant-style cuisine) is de rigueur when dining in Siena and central Tuscany. Signature 'poor dishes' in the area are vegetarian-friendly, such as the stewy bread-and-vegetable-based *ribollita*. The prototypical Sienese pasta is *pici* – rustic 'fat spaghetti', often dressed *all'aglione* (*aglione* is a large, bulbous, garlic-esque vegetable from the Val di Chiana). *Gnudi senesi* or *malfatti* are divine spinach and ricotta dumplings, while the *cinta senese* (p94), a pig species native to the area, forms the base of many appetiser boards. Sweet treats (p84), Vernaccia wine from San Gimignano and wines from the Chianti Senese (p82) are other highlights.

Best coffee and sweets
Caffè Nannini (p86)

Must-try wines
Enoteca I Terzi (p102)

CONNECT & FIND YOUR WAY

Wi-fi Siena's free network is ComunediSiena Wi-fi; coverage includes most of the areas around key attractions – but it's spotty.

Navigation Siena's centre is closed to unauthorised cars, though there are several car parks just outside the city gates. For countryside navigation, renting a car is the best option – dealing with the Autolinee Toscane bus lines and limited stops can be tricky.

STAY UP-TO-DATE

Terredisiena.it is an official platform run by the Tuscan Region and several institutional partners, frequently updated in English with interesting events.

WHERE TO STAY

As tourism returns post-pandemic, accommodation rates are soaring, but there are still deals to be had, whether you're looking for an urban apartment, *agriturismo* (farm stay) or traditional *albergo* (hotel).

City	Pro/Con
Siena	A jewel of a Gothic city with plenty of activity outside the main tourist circuit. Heaving with crowds in high season.
Montalcino	A wine lovers' mecca, beloved for Brunello, but not much beyond that in terms of activity.
Volterra	Fascinating Etruscan history; overabundance of vampire-fiction enthusiasts!

MONEY

As part of the Covid-era National Recovery & Resilience Plan, merchants are required to accept point-of-sale (POS) payments by card, but it's still good local form to have small change on hand for things like quick bar and cafe purchases and on-the-spot tickets.

09 Discovering the
DUOMO

CATHEDRAL | PANORAMAS | TOURS

Siena's Santa Maria Assunta cathedral is gargantuan, a Gothic-Romanesque powerhouse. It's also a rare example of a sacred monument where the interior meets – or exceeds – the high expectations created by the ornate facade. Star-studded vaults, a Nicola Pisano–carved marble pulpit and hefty striped pillars compete for your attention. Feeling gobsmacked here is standard.

GIMAS/SHUTTERSTOCK ©

🗺 How to

Tickets The **Opera della Metropolitana di Siena** (operaduomosiena.it) oversees the complex. The OPA Si Pass is valid for three days and grants admission to the cathedral, baptistery, Museo dell'Opera, Piccolomini Library, Facciatone and crypt.

Add-ons A special Porta del Cielo (Gate of Heaven) itinerary and guided tours of the cathedral floors are available seasonally.

When to go During 'pavimento season', typically late June to late July and mid-August to mid-October, the protective floor covering is removed, unveiling intricate mosaics.

POLUDZIBER/SHUTTERSTOCK ©

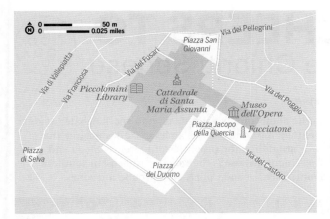

Top left Piccolomini Library
Bottom left Facciatone

Magnificent manuscripts While the Cattedrale di Santa Maria Assunta is the centrepiece, its offshoots and surrounding structures amp up the intrigue. A detour through an unassuming door on the north aisle of the cathedral will turn your vision technicolour. The **Piccolomini Library** was constructed for Pius II's collection of illuminated manuscripts, and while its wraparound display offers a succinct overview of the tradition, it's the colour-saturated frescoes by Pinturicchio and the gold-flecked, grotesque-gilded ceiling that most inspire the eye (and, likely, the Instagram post).

Siena from above Outside, if you're facing the cathedral head-on, the **Facciatone** is the stark and comparatively threadbare structure to the right. It's a remnant of an attempted expansion of the church that began in the 14th century, but was thwarted, then definitively stopped, by the Black Plague and its fallout. Today the Facciatone – roughly translated as 'big facade' – is Siena's panoramic lookout par excellence (with a 131-step climb to the top). Many Duomo ticket holders skip it, however, as it doesn't look readily scalable at a glance.

Don't-miss Duccio With all the sensory overload of the cathedral itself, bypassing the **Museo dell'Opera** might seem excusable – but Duccio di Buoninsegna's monumental *Maestà* altarpiece (1331) is a must. Intended for the high altar of the cathedral, it was an important transitional work, helping to set the stage for early Renaissance painting.

🏠 Unique Cathedral Tours

During July and August, the OPA and Opera Laboratori (operalaboratori. com) organise a series of by-reservation-only nighttime and early-morning visits to the cathedral. There's the 'Lux in Nocte' tour, an after-sunset, by-flashlight adventure, during which details can be seen from a new perspective. 'Tra Cielo e Terra' is a guided exploration of the cathedral floors from an on-high viewpoint, while 'Good Morning Siena' is a wake-up call with the custodians as they turn on the lights and prepare the space for the day's pilgrims. Spots fill quickly and and dates aren't always given on the OPA website; your best bet is to contact the Siena office of Opera Laboratori at opera.siena@ operalaboratori.com.

10 CHEERS TO
the Chianti Senese

WINE | VINEYARDS | DRINKING

Ah, Chianti: though the name and its variants tend to spark debate (among oenophiles) or confusion (among the wine-curious amateur), all can agree that the wine production region – straddling the provinces of Florence, Siena and Arezzo – is pure poetry. The Chianti Senese is the roughly 400-sq-km southern section, encompassing Chianti Classico and Colli Senesi production zones.

STEVANZZ/GETTY IMAGES ©

⟨ How to

Getting around While some bus routes on the Autolinee Toscane–Siena Extraurbano circuit (at-bus.it) stop off in key Chianti towns, reaching individual wineries is much simpler by car. Start on the Strada Statale 674 from Siena.

When to go Autumn is the most appealing season, for colours and temperatures but also for fairs linked to the *vendemmia* (harvest).

Tasting etiquette Most wineries don't pocket much from small group tastings. Post-tasting, plan to buy a few bottles or to place an order.

FANI KURTI/GETTY IMAGES ©

Top left Vineyard, Castellina in Chianti
Bottom left Wine tasting, Chianti

Know the region Gaiole in Chianti, Radda in Chianti, Castelnuovo Berardenga and Castellina in Chianti are the Chianti Senese's four main municipalities, each home to wineries, remote hamlets and artistic or cultural cachet. Rivers from the Ambra to the Pesa move southeast through the area, but, more importantly, the wines flow in every direction.

Ama: a time capsule of a town Run by Lorenza Sebasti and Marco Pallanti, the **Castello di Ama** estate produces well-respected wines, including the world-famous L'Apparita merlot, along with lesser-known but equally worthwhile pours like a summery Tuscan IGT pinot noir. The unconventional on-site sculpture park, which features the likes of French-American artist Louise Bourgeois, sets it apart from other wineries.

Sculpture and cycling heritage Still within the municipality of Gaiole in Chianti, in the hamlet La Fornace, the sprawling **Chianti Sculpture Park** is open year-round and shows contemporary works by local and international artists. **Gaiole in Chianti** proper, a 15-minute drive away, is also the start and finish line of the beloved L'Eroica bicycle race (p104), which runs from the first Sunday of October each year.

Historic Castellina wines The wine scene in sleepy Castellina in Chianti was shaped by the noble Squarcialupi family, whose namesake *palazzo* is now a hotel located not far from **La Castellina**, a well-known wine estate with a direct-sales outpost on Viale della Rimembranza. Interestingly, the local **Museo Archeologico del Chianti Senese** exhibits artefacts that far predate the Squarcialupi family, including from the Bronze Age and Etruscan period.

 Taste the Chianti Colli Senesi

La Torre alle Tolfe is a winery, restaurant and villa accommodation just minutes from the centre of Siena, in the DOCG Chianti Colli Senesi territory. Grapes that were traditionally blended to make 'Chianti' are now holding their own, unblended, enjoying the spotlight in *purezza*. Schedule a tasting at La Torre alle Tolfe and you'll learn about the grapes and the wines, see why they are capable of going solo and understand their place within the original Chianti context.

 ■ Recommended by **Emily O'Hare,** *WSET course instructor, wine writer and sommelier in Siena* @emilyohwine

11 **SWEET**
Treats in Town

DESSERT | SWEETS | FESTIVALS

Tiramisu and gelato aside, dessert doesn't tend to be the standout course at most Italian tables. In Tuscany, though, and especially Siena, that stereotype is put to the test. From the Christmastime *panforte* to sugar-dusted *ricciarelli,* the town has confectionery traditions that stretch back centuries.

🗺 How to

Carnival season Sweet-toothed travellers will be spoilt for choice during Carnival season, a prelude to the Christian liturgical time of Lent, which runs from late January to around mid-March.

Sweet souvenirs With a shelf life of several months, *panforte* makes a great holiday gift. It's typically beautifully packaged in eye-catching, medieval-style wrapping paper, and this 'strong bread' should stay in one piece when you travel.

SIENA & CENTRAL TUSCANY EXPERIENCES

Panforte

Literally translated as 'strong bread', this spiced dessert cake made with candied and dried fruits, honey, pepper and other spices is a Siena stalwart, as emblematic of the area as the Palio or its host piazza. Though it's traditionally eaten during the Christmas season, it's sought-after enough, particularly by culinary-curious visitors, that you can find it in Siena year-round. Expect to see it in two distinct iterations: one 'black', when the external coating is spice-based, and one 'white', when it's sugary. Both fit *panforte*'s exacting PGI (Protected Geographical Indication) production standards.

Panforte's roots are in the pepper- and honey-rich breads of medieval times; in particular, one record dating to the early 13th century suggests it originated as a table gift

🍰 Other Sweets

Ricciarelli Soft but never crumbly, these treats first appeared in the 14th century and little about the recipe has changed since.

Amaretti Traditionally made with ground almonds, with a balance of bitter and sweet.

Cantuccini Crisp and crunchy *cantuccini*, paired with Vin Santo ('holy wine'), are a quintessentially Tuscan way to top off a meal.

Above left *Panforte*
Above right *Amaretti* **Left** *Ricciarelli*

for nuns in the Siena province's Abbey of Montecelso. But the first-known manufacturer of *panforte di Siena* wasn't founded until the 19th century. While precise facts and figures for the spice-coated 'black' version are elusive, the 'white' version as it's currently known is linked to an 1879 visit from Queen Margherita, who was served this twist on the traditional recipe while she was in town for the August Palio.

Getting a proper *panforte* education can be as simple as perusing local bakeries, cafes and traditional product shops – Caffè Nannini is a solid start, as is the historic **Antica Drogheria Manganelli** (p105). But if you really want to spice things up (forgive us), the **Fabbrica del Panforte** (fabbricadelpanforte.com), where you can get a firsthand look at (and scent of!) the production process, is about a 15-minute drive from the city centre. Owner and head of operations Fausto Leoncini is passionate

☕ Caffè Nannini

This old-school corner bar and *pasticceria* (Via Banchi di Sopra 24), lined floor to ceiling with typical Sienese sweets for sale, is a must for your morning cappuccino and pastry. Still run by the namesake family that started the business in the early 20th century, Nannini's good-humoured staff, swanky wraparound marble countertops and ample seating all encourage lingering. And linger, you should, whether it's over an early-morning espresso or an after-dinner *amaro*.

Note that at Nannini, it's not so much about hot-from-the-oven delights as it is stocking up on Sienese sweet loot. House-produced treats, from *panforte* predecessor *panpepato* to *cavallucci* – tough, anise-and-walnut wonder cookies once associated with horseback travellers – are all prettily packaged and make stellar souvenirs or gifts.

ANDREA PISTOLESI/GETTY IMAGES ©

Left Sweets including *panforte*, *panpepato* and *cavallucci*, Caffè Nannini **Below** *Frittelle di San Giuseppe*

about pushing the Sienese sweet tradition forward and will coordinate visits for curious groups if contacted.

Frittelle di San Giuseppe

During Carnival season, a buffet of season-specific baked and fried sweet treats surface in Tuscan shop windows, *pasticceria* displays and home parties. In Siena, *frittelle di San Giuseppe* are among the most highly anticipated delights: golden-fried, sugar-coated, orange-scented rice fritters, clunkily translated as 'St Joseph's fritters'. You'll see them in excess on and around 19 March, which is both the feast day of St Joseph and Italian Father's Day.

Siena's *frittelle* are special not for their unusual ingredients, but for how they're served. Typically, from the last Saturday in January until the Sunday after St Joseph's Day, the local Savelli family sets up a kiosk smack-dab in the middle of **Piazza del Campo**, dishing out piping-hot *frittelle,* and have been doing so for over a century. The final product is crunchy on the outside, creamy on the inside and with frying grease lightly staining the crisp paper bag in which it's distributed.

The Savelli family aren't professional cooks, and indeed have a range of 'regular jobs', but they share another hyperlocal family passion when off duty: breeding horses for the Palio (p96).

SONIA62/GETTY IMAGES ©

12
The Gothic City's
GREENERY

GARDENS | OUTDOORS | HISTORY

After enough time amid its steep streets, hulking *palazzi* and surplus of stone, Siena can get you pining for green space and crowd-free corners. But you don't have to venture far to find a breath of fresh air. The city centre has a sprinkling of natural refuges, with deep roots and rich layered histories.

Above Orto de' Pecci **Right** Orto Botanico dell'Università di Siena (p90)

🗺 How to

Getting around Orto de' Pecci is easily reached on foot from the historic centre. If you're driving in from out of town, there's free parking at the on-site restaurant.

When to go If you visit Orto de' Pecci during the restaurant's idle between-meal mo-

ments, you're likely to find students sprawled on the grass, kids and parents mingling with the farm animals and picnicking friends divvying out their bounties atop blankets.

Pit stop On the way back up to the heart of the historic centre from Orto de' Pecci, stop off at Tea Room (p102).

Orto de' Pecci

Given the compact nature of Siena's city centre, the sheer size of the Pecci is impressive. This herb-scented oasis offers the ultimate comedown from the chaos of high-season Piazza del Campo – and quite literally, too. The walk to this sprawling community garden is mostly on a winding yet steady decline from Palazzo Pubblico.

The park was once a residential neighbourhood with dozens of homes and small-community staples such as a church and local businesses until the Plague wiped it out in 1348. Later it took on a more ominous guise as the passageway to the **Porta di Giustizia**, where condemned prisoners were sent for execution.

Today there's the on-site **Ristorante All'Orto de' Pecci** with hearty home cooking

(try the *pici* with wild fennel *ragù*), a model medieval garden that's now used for educational workshops with local school groups, an 'animal village' complete with peacocks and donkeys, plus a smattering of art installations and seasonal concerts.

Orto Botanico dell'Università di Siena

The tropical-looking trees at the entrance to this 2.5-hectare, university-owned garden may momentarily transport you out of Siena, but you're still within the city's medieval walls – and in a hyperlocal, historical place, at that. Like many fixtures of Sienese culture, the Orto Botanico has a distinct link to Santa Maria della Scala. It's an outgrowth of the Giardino dei Semplici, which, in the late 16th century, was annexed to the hospital and served as the cultivation centre for medicinal plants. When Grand Duke of Tuscany Pietro Leopoldo called for a university-wide reform in 1784, the plant collection was expanded, with some 900 rare plant species already in its records.

In 1856 the university's botanical garden headquarters were transferred to the current centre, just at the edge of the medieval walls, but an easy five-minute walk from its

📖 Orto de' Pecci's Past Life

The seeds for Orto de' Pecci's current setup were planted in 1983, after a decree known as the Basaglia law reformed Italy's mental healthcare system, calling for, among other things, the shutdown of psychiatric hospitals. Since the 19th century, Siena's local hospital had been using the garden as an occupational therapy site; its fruits and vegetables were used to feed hospital guests. As hospital staff questioned what would happen to their most vulnerable patients, an idea to create a work cooperative was born. Today the co-op has expanded and now integrates workers coming through a variety of hardships, from people who have been formerly incarcerated to those readjusting to civic life after inpatient drug rehabilitation.

The Orto Botanico's Ghost

Siena native and former foreign correspondent Annalisa Coppolaro is the author of *Luoghi Arcani*, a book about the city's potentially haunted spaces. Annalisa cautions visitors to be on the lookout for 'Giomo', the Orto Botanico's alleged ghost, particularly when it's raining. Reports of the garden watchmen have been surfacing since the 1940s.

FEDERICO MAGONIO/SHUTTERSTOCK ©

old home in Santa Maria della Scala. Over the years, the garden has come under the care of varied departments of 'UniSi': first the medicine and surgery faculty, later the pharmacy school, and, still today, the faculty of mathematics, physics and natural sciences.

After winding your way through the more than 1000 plant species spread around the garden, you can dip into the **Museum of Natural History**, housed within the still-active research centre of the Accademia dei Fisiocritici. It's a mystical-feeling museum, a strange blend of the scientific and the spiritual, since the museums are housed in a former Camaldolese monastery from the 12th century.

Back in the garden, three distinct greenhouses set amid the rows charm in different ways: the tepidarium, with its frequent contemporary art exhibitions; the serra, or greenhouse proper, with its gallery of succulents; and the orangerie, with its space carved out for carnivorous plants. Later additions like the rock garden, a sloping escarpment and a calming lake lend the landscape balance.

LEFT: WILL PERRETT/ALAMY STOCK PHOTO © FAR LEFT: FEDERICO MAGONIO/SHUTTERSTOCK ©

Left Orto de' Pecci **Top** Museum of Natural History **Above** Orto Botanico dell'Università di Siena

13

San Gimignano
JAUNT

DAY TRIP | CONTEMPORARY ART | ARCHITECTURE

▬▬▬ Referred to as the Town of 100 Towers and the Manhattan of the Middle Ages, San Gimignano is charmingly contradictory. While this walled village maintains its medieval exterior, contemporary flavour and a spirit of invention also come through.

CANADASTOCK/SHUTTERSTOCK ©

🖼 Art & Sculpture

Arte all'Arte A public project of permanent artworks spread about town.

Ombra di San Gimignano An exemplary work of early Hellenistic sculpture on view at the Archaeological Museum.

Palazzo Comunale The Supreme Poet got his own namesake room, the Sala Dante, after he visited here in 1299.

🗺 Trip Notes

Getting around Buses to San Gimignano depart regularly from the Poggibonsi train station, easily reached from Siena. Once you're here, explore on foot.

When to go October is beautiful, but everyone's caught on. November still has the autumnal appeal, with fewer crowds (and more fickle weather).

■ Recommended by Phoebe Owston,
Communications and Social Media Manager at Galleria Continua
@phoebeowston

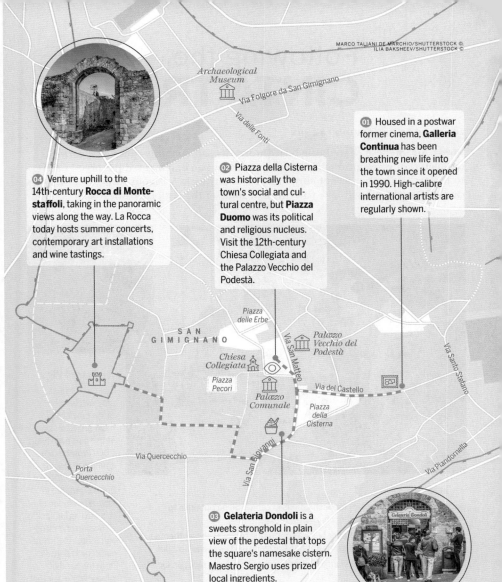

Archaeological Museum

Via Folgore da San Gimignano

Via delle Fonti

01 Housed in a postwar former cinema, **Galleria Continua** has been breathing new life into the town since it opened in 1990. High-calibre international artists are regularly shown.

04 Venture uphill to the 14th-century **Rocca di Monte-staffoli**, taking in the panoramic views along the way. La Rocca today hosts summer concerts, contemporary art installations and wine tastings.

02 Piazza della Cisterna was historically the town's social and cultural centre, but **Piazza Duomo** was its political and religious nucleus. Visit the 12th-century Chiesa Collegiata and the Palazzo Vecchio del Podestà.

SAN GIMIGNANO

Piazza delle Erbe

Via San Matteo

Palazzo Vecchio del Podestà

Chiesa Collegiata

Piazza Pecori

Palazzo Comunale

Via del Castello

Via Santo Stefano

Piazza della Cisterna

Via Quercecchio

Via San Giovanni

Porta Quercecchio

Via Piandornella

03 **Gelateria Dondoli** is a sweets stronghold in plain view of the pedestal that tops the square's namesake cistern. Maestro Sergio uses prized local ingredients.

Gelateria Dondoli

N

0 — 100 m
0 — 0.05 miles

Following the
CINTA TRAIL

LOCAL FOOD | SHOPPING | TOURS

Any Sienese charcuterie board worth its salt contains sausage, *rigatino* (pancetta) or prosciutto made from *cinta senese,* an endangered pig breed native to the area. Whether or not cured meat – or any meat – is your thing, following a *cinta*-themed trail will take you through some of the region's tastiest spots.

VALERY RIZZO/ALAMY STOCK PHOTO ©

🗺 Trip Notes

Getting around Stay on foot for destinations in central Siena but drive to Tenuta di Spannocchia (spannocchia.com).

When to go March and November bring a smattering of *cinta senese*–themed *sagre* (local food festivals) to towns like San Casciano dei Bagni and Sovicille.

Dining out Look out for *ragù bianco di cinta Senese* (white-wine *ragù*) on local menus.

🐖 Prized Pigs

The *cinta senese* may well be the Siena province's most prized resident. These pigs have had PDO (Protected Designation of Origin) status since 2006, but are believed to have been raised in this area as far back as Roman and Etruscan times. The name *cinta* (belt) derives from the band of silvery-white hair that wraps around their black coats.

02 Consorzio di Agrario Siena is your one-stop gourmet goods shop: pick up cured *cinta senese* salami or prosciutto, aged *pecorino* from the Crete Senesi or an easy *panino*.

○Le Scotte

Siena

03 As the Siena province's longest-running deli (since 1931), **Antica Salumeria Salvini** concentrates mainly on *cinta senese* cold cuts.

Riserva Naturale Alto Merse

○Sovicille

Ampugnano
○

San Rocco a Pilli
○

01 In the Sala dei Nove at **Museo Civico**, Ambrogio Lorenzetti's *Allegory of Good and Bad Government* fresco cycle (p100; undergoing restoration at time of writing) features the first-known artistic rendering of the *cinta senese*.

C E N T R A L
T U S C A N Y

○Rosia

04 The sprawling organic farm **Tenuta di Spannocchia** (and *agriturismo;* pictured left) offers a hands-on Cinta Senese Experience, which includes following the pigs through their free-range pastures and a tasting of delectable cured meats.

0 — 2 km
0 — 1 miles

Palio Pageantry

SIENA'S DEFINITIVE AND PROUD TRADITION

In many dry heat-heavy, tree-starved towns of Tuscany, July and August – high season for both tourists and temperatures – can be tough. It's the time of year when many residents skip town for the coast. Much of Siena's local population soldiers on, though, their daily activity and neighbourhood pride going into overdrive in preparation for the Palio.

Above left Palio di Siena
Middle *Contrada* flags **Right** Piazza del Campo during the Palio

MIGEL/SHUTTERSTOCK ©

The Backdrop & Build-up

Palio – the wild horse race pitting 10 of the city's 17 *contrade* (town districts) against each other, every year on 2 July and 16 August. The horses? Bareback. The heat? Scorching. The drama unfolds in the shell-shaped, sharply curved Piazza del Campo. The dates, in fact, are the only predictable element of the Palio, a spectacle of the highest order, equal parts artful and borderline barbaric.

Piazza del Campo, with its sloping sides and imposing architecture, is as integral to the Palio as the horses or jockeys themselves. (Each jockey-horse pair, by the way, has its first interaction only a few days before each race). The tension is discernible, visceral, calling for a cinematic setting. But it's not just this stage that sets the mood. Representatives from each *contrada,* ceremoniously called *contradaioli,* parade through town in costume, carrying their banners. Marching musicians in matching garb confirm the seriousness of the enterprise to any sceptics. Amid all the waiting around, spectators' eyes are bound to wander, taking in the Torre del Mangia (p101) rather than a jumbotron. There's pomp, there's circumstance, there are preparatory dances of horses and jockeys. Then it's all over in a minute – if that.

Safety concerns expressed by activists usually involve the animals, but it's arguably the jockeys who are risking more – if they get bucked off in those fateful seconds, the crowd's attention probably won't be on them: officially their horse can still win. Beyond gloating rights and ritualistic pride, the winning district receives the *drappellone,* a silk flag hand-painted by a different artist each year.

DELPIXEL/SHUTTERSTOCK ©

CULTURA RM EXCLUSIVE/FABIO MUZZI/GETTY IMAGES ©

Second-place trophies have no place here, and rankings of final timings aren't released in any official capacity. At the Palio, data doesn't matter; the *drappellone* does.

Background & Comeback

Seventeen of Siena's original 59 *contrade* still exist and are eligible to compete. All 17 have a symbol, but 'She-Wolf, Unicorn, Dragon, Panther and Goose' makes a nice representative sample. How the 10 competing *contrade* are chosen is a Sienese science best not broken too far down; suffice to say, it involves a fanfare-heavy drawing by the mayor, begun with trumpet blasts. The roots of the race itself are medieval – or, as Palio chronicler Orlando Papei puts it, 'remote' – but the event has 'only' run continuously since 1633. Some regulations still in place today were drawn up that first documented year. These days, 2 July and 16 August are firmer fixtures on the local calendar than any national holiday or halfheartedly-patriotic festivity. Until 2020, the only years where the Palio was ever thwarted were during the First and Second World Wars. But when Covid-19 hit and Italy's intensive restrictions went into place, the Palio was off the table for the better part of three years. In the emotional return on 2 July 2022, the Dragon took home the honours.

> There's pomp, there's circumstance, there are preparatory dances of horses and jockeys. Then it's all over in a minute – if that.

🐎 Taking Part

Palio purists – so, most Sienese residents – stubbornly defend the race's integrity. Despite the theatricality, they insist this is not commercial entertainment for visitors but the long-flowing lifeblood of the city. And they're right. Still, the hotel markups and expensive, hard-won seats in bleachers, or on select cafe terraces, are something curious outsiders should plan for. (You can brave the standing-room-only ring in the middle of the Campo, but it requires several hours to jostle for a space).

While true race days are mired in pandemonium, trial runs take place quietly, often just after sunrise, in the days leading up to the main event. Getting a glimpse of those practices lends insight to all the exacting energy, all the rigid control and regulation, behind the proceedings. Still, there's no stand-in for the raucousness of the real thing.

15 Countryside Gothic
RELICS

ARCHITECTURE | HISTORY | LANDSCAPES

There's hardly a better place to connect with heaven than an abandoned, roofless abbey that opens up to the sky in the middle of the Senese countryside. Even those not so spiritually inclined will stand in awe under the majestic apse of the 800-year-old Abbazia di San Galgano – the first Gothic church built in Tuscany – located near the legendary Eremo di Montesiepi.

SIENA & CENTRAL TUSCANY EXPERIENCES

BUFFY1982/SHUTTERSTOCK ©

🗺 How to

Getting here From Siena, follow the Strada Provinciale 73 bis for 35 minutes. Turn right at the brown sign pointing to San Galgano.

Tickets Entrance to the complex costs €5, which includes access to the Museo Civico e Diocesano d'Arte Sacra in Chiusdino. Family tickets are available for €15.

Opening hours San Galgano is open from 9am daily. Closing times range from 5.30pm to 8pm, depending on the season.

DEA/G. COZZI/DE AGOSTINI VIA GETTY IMAGES ©

Eremo di Montesiepi It's hard to imagine what knight Galgano Guidotti (1148–1181) felt when he first set foot in Montesiepi in the late 12th century to live the rest of his life in isolation, renouncing his violent past as the Archangel Michael commanded in a dream. The round, Romanesque chapel completed here in 1185 on the site where the warrior turned monk retired as a hermit is still functioning. A short hike will take you under its black-and-white dome where mass is held every Sunday amid the frescoes of 14th-century Sienese painter Ambrogio Lorenzetti.

Abbazia di San Galgano As numerous miracles were attributed to Galgano during the canonisation process (1185), more and more pilgrims began reaching Montesiepi. In 1218 the Cistercian monks that had settled in the area began erecting a 1500-sq-metre abbey below the hermitage to cater for the saint's growing fanbase. The project would take 70 years to complete. Walking towards the abbey's facade amid neatly planted cypress trees offers a spectacular perspective on its unique architecture, but only by entering the structure can you marvel at the intricate stonework and picture the medieval celebrations once held in such picturesque scenery.

An abbey without a roof There is no shortage of breathtaking churches in Tuscany, but what makes the Abbazia di San Galgano especially photogenic is the absence of a roof. The abbey was abandoned by monks in the 15th century and in 1786 lightning struck the bell tower, which fell flat on the roof causing it to collapse.

Top left Abbazia di San Galgano **Bottom left** Iron sword, Eremo di Montesiepi

 Tuscany's Own Excalibur

As you enter the hermitage, you'll notice the hilt of an old iron sword sticking out from a rock in front of the altar. Tale has it that when Galgano first moved to Montesiepi he inserted his sword in a stone as a symbolic gesture to demonstrate his willingness to give up arms and dedicate the rest of his days to God. It is around the mythical weapon – now contained in a shrine to protect it against King Arthur wannabes – that the circular Eremo was built after the knight's death.

SIENA'S
Icons

01 The Duomo's floor panels
Giorgio Vasari proclaimed these marble inlay and graffito floors 'the most magnificent ever made'. Protected for most of the year, they're unveiled for a limited time twice a year (p81).

02 Ciaccino senese
Foreigners (ahem, Florentines) would call it *schiacciata*, but the Sienese doggedly stick to their semantics. Whatever characteristics *ciaccino* may share with its rival, it's a mainstay of local street food.

03 Cinta senese
A domestic pig bred only in the Siena territory, the *cinta senese* (p94) is steeped in mythology and carries the distinguished PDO (Protected Designation of Origin) status.

04 Allegory of Good and Bad Government
Ambrogio Lorenzetti's signature fresco cycle in Siena's Palazzo Civico was commissioned by the city's Council of Nine (naturally, they're depicted on the 'Good Government' side).

05 Torre del Mangia
Standing guard over Piazza del Campo, the Torre del Mangia inspires every second souvenir magnet sold around town. It remains one of Italy's tallest secular towers.

06 Lanterns
She-wolves and dragons and fish, oh my! Colourful street lamps with the symbol of each *contrada* are used to demarcate the historic districts.

07 The drappellone
The hand-painted silk flag awarded to the winning *contrada* at the close of the Palio (p96). Locals affectionately call it the *cencio* (rag).

08 Duccio di Buoninsegna's Maestà
This massive altarpiece by one of Siena's most renowned artists helped usher in a new era of Italian art – one without the constraints of Byzantine conventions.

09 Ricciarelli
These whimsical marzipan delights are a holiday-season staple in Siena, but iconic enough to appear in bakery windows and bow-wrapped boxes year-round.

Listings

BEST OF THE REST

✕ Home-Style Cooking

Osteria il Grattacielo   €

The workers at this ramshackle deli are as good-humoured as the name of the space would imply. (*Il grattacielo* translates to 'the skyscraper', but most average Joes could touch the low ceilings here.) There's no menu, just a no-frills countertop with rotating dishes.

Osteria La Sosta di Violante   €

A reliable nice-priced trattoria on Via del Pantaneto where you'll usually be able to get seated on the fly. Both the *paccheri* (tube pasta) with *cinta senese* sauce and the extra-warm waiters are memorable.

Osteria Babazuf   €

Tuscan dishes have a contemporary streak here, and the kitchen staff, a knack for presentation. Seafood options are the standouts; try the octopus served with salsa verde and sweet-sour marinated red cabbage.

Osteria Le Logge   €€

This local favourite, housed in a converted pharmacy, still spills over with Sienese. Given the old-school trattoria fare and the cosy, book-lined dining area, Le Logge feels a bit like eating at the home of the coolest neighbourhood nonna.

Trattoria La Tellina   €

Don't be put off by the red-check tablecloths: La Tellina is not a cookie-cutter tourist joint. The cramped-yet-convivial dining area and peek-a-boo lace curtains on the doors lends this local stalwart an at-home ambience.

☕ Cosy Spots in Siena

Tea Room

Tea Room is both cosmopolitan and comfy. Find a seat on one of the sofas for an Indian tea and splashy iced chai, or on the outdoor terrace for a bird's-eye view of the Porta di Giustizia (Gate of Justice) and the green surroundings.

Enoteca I Terzi

This elegant hole-in-the-wall is housed in a 12th-century tower known alternately as the Torre dell'Orsa (Bear Tower) and the Ballanti (Dancers). You won't find either, but you will find a lengthy list of regional wines and a comfy ambience.

Caffè Fiorella

Opened by its namesake three decades ago and now run by her son Francesco, Caffè Fiorella is a nifty breakfast spot not far from the Campo chaos. It's not just a bar but a roastery, rich in artisanal coffee and tempting pastries.

Caffè Fiorella

🏛 Major Museums & Monuments

Santa Maria della Scala

This former hospital is the definitive site for understanding Siena's place as a stop on the Via Francigena pilgrimage road. Particularly key is the Pellegrinaio (Pilgrims' Hall) upstairs, home to 15th-century frescoes paying tribute to the hospital's vocation.

Pinacoteca Nazionale

Get up close with the Sienese school of Simone Martini, Duccio di Buoninsegna and their contemporaries. This glittering painting gallery is a testament to why Siena is better remembered for its Gothic and medieval triumphs than Florentine Renaissance–style feats.

Chiesa di San Domenico

Those following the trail of St Catherine of Siena will want to view the only true portrait of her, painted by Andrea Vanni and housed in a west-end chapel at this former Dominican oratory.

San Clemente in Santa Maria dei Servi

With its rustic facade, this Piazza Manzoni stronghold is nothing to speak of from the outside, but wander in and you'll find Coppo di Marcovaldo's Late Byzantine–style *Madonna del Bordone,* easily the neighbourhood highlight.

🏛 Niche Museums & Smaller Monuments

Museo delle Tavolette di Biccherna

This museum holds 100-plus painted tablets – some decorated by iconic Sienese artists – that were used as covers for the registers and administrative records of the Biccherna, the financial magistrate during the 13th and 14th centuries.

DENIS VOSTRIKOV/SHUTTERSTOCK ©

Chiesa di San Domenico

Museo dell'Acqua

This multimedia museum – in view of the magical Pescaia Fountains and open only upon reservation – features centuries-old Siena artefacts and ruins, along with documents and films highlighting how the *bottini* system (a network of underground aqueducts) shaped civic life.

Synagogue and Jewish Museum

Siena's synagogue stands in the old Jewish ghetto, where the local population remained confined until 1859 – nearly 300 years after Cosimo I de' Medici first extended Florence's restrictive measures (p138). Today it's the heartbeat of the vibrant local Jewish community.

Casa di Santa Caterina

St Catherine's House, converted into a grand sanctuary in 1466, was the religious icon's birthplace, not to mention home to her two dozen siblings.

Musei delle Contrade

Each *contrada* (historic district) of Siena has its own museum where they proudly display the *drapelloni* (Palio flags) that they've won over the years, along with memorabilia and tall tales of past wins. Most require reservations to visit.

Palazzo Tolomei

Palazzo Tolomei was the headquarters of local government prior to Palazzo Civico. But it's more famous for the stories swirling around noblewoman Pia Tolomei, allegedly murdered by her Guelph husband and mentioned in Dante's *Purgatory*.

Palazzo dei Diavoli

Just outside the Porta Camollia, one of the old city gates, this unassuming brick building, dubbed Devils' Palace, is a favourite among local tellers of supernatural tales, who link it to possible 'diabolic intervention' in the Sienese victory of 1526 at the Battle of Porta Camollia.

Other Museums Around Siena

Crystal Museum in Colle Val d'Elsa

Deep dive into Colle Val d'Elsa's long crystal and glass tradition, which began with one transplanted French glassmaker. Today this off-the-map Tuscan town produces 15% of the world's crystal.

Raffaele de Grada Gallery of Modern & Contemporary Art

Housed in the former Santa Chiara monastery in San Gimignano, this space is certainly no Galleria Continua (p93), but it does shine a nice spotlight on 19th-century Tuscan painting traditions.

Etruscan Museum of Guarnacci

This museum in Volterra holds an impressive collection of Etruscan urns but is most famous for housing the quasi-eerie, elongated bronze statue *Ombra della Sera* (Shadow of the Evening).

Ecomuseum of Alabaster

Explore the long-standing relationship between Volterra, its community and this rich, precious rock. The museum highlights sculptures but also traces the evolution of alabaster from the Etruscan period to the present day.

Markets, Festivals & Events

Mercato nel Campo

A Christmas-season marketplace usually held on the first weekend of December in Siena. Its 150-plus, medieval-style stalls positively overflow with tempting goods and stocking stuffers to send home.

MICAT in Vertice

The varied musical season of the Accademia Musicale Chigiana di Siena typically runs from November to June, kicking off on 22 November with the feast of Cecilia, patron saint of musicians.

Sausage Walk: Il Mondo dei Bassotti (The World of Dachshunds)

Introduced in 2018 after a similar initiative cropped up in Milan, this annual dachshund strut through town, orchestrated by the humans who love them, isn't quite on par with the Palio yet. But it makes for its own quirky September spectacle.

Volterragusto

Volterra's postcard-perfect Piazza dei Priori is the HQ of this white truffle festival held in autumn, featuring newly pressed oil, truffles and wines, plus an amusing cheese-rolling competition, the Palio dei Caci.

DEAGOSTINI/GETTY IMAGES ©

Etruscan Museum of Guarnacci

L'Eroica

This vintage-flavoured bicycle race in Gaiole is Chianti's signature event, held on the first Sunday of October and starting and finishing in the whimsical wine town.

Siena Wednesday Market

Every Wednesday morning, stalls sprawl out around the Medici Fortress and the stadium. It's a fun everyday-grocery stop and buried treasures are scattered among the clothing racks and bins.

Vernaccia di San Gimignano DOCG

 ## Craft Hotspots in Siena

Ceramiche Artistiche Santa Caterina

This inspiring, multi-generational workshop sells fine works from the Neri family, who carried out ceramics studies in the 'capital' of Montelupo Fiorentino.

Il Pellicano

Local ceramicist Elisabetta Ricci's shop has been operating for going on 40 years now. Many items feature typical designs depicting the Tuscan countryside, but others are more Siena-specific: think *contrada*-themed dishes and door knockers.

 ## Sienese Bites, Bells & Whistles

Antica Drogheria Manganelli

Bustling since 1879, Manganelli teems with iconic Tuscan and Italian treats. The loose candies, potpourri and teas in glass cases and pharmacy-style containers beg to be photographed; walls are lined top to bottom with *panforte*, mints and Martelli pasta bags.

La Boutique del Caffè

Moka pots and French presses of all stripes and sizes line the shelves at this speciality shop, but it's the coffees, teas and candies from around the world that really merit attention. Stock up on artisanal jams, exotic *tisane* and lesser-known coffee labels from Italy and beyond.

Galleria Novecento

Emanuele Pianigiani's hip vintage-themed gallery will woo aesthetes with a penchant for canonical Italian film posters, nostalgic ad campaigns and fanciful household objects.

 ## Non-Chianti Wine Denominations

Vernaccia di San Gimignano DOCG

Dating back to the Middle Ages, Vernaccia is Tuscany's premier white grape, with the body and personality to back it up, and less fruitier notes than comparable whites.

Brunello di Montalcino DOCG

Strictly Sangiovese, this ruby-red with notes of berries and cherries is a regional icon and reputed as the Italian red with the greatest longevity, besides Barolo.

Rosso di Montepulciano DOC

Another red to watch for in the wineries and restaurant menus of the region, Rosso di Montepulciano DOC is dry but never dull.

Scan to find more things to do in Siena & Central Tuscany online

SIENA & CENTRAL TUSCANY REVIEWS

VAL D'ORCIA

COUNTRYSIDE | WINE | RURAL HAMLETS

Experience
Val d'Orcia
online

Don't miss the monastic complex of the **Abbazia di Monte Oliveto Maggiore** near Asciano (p119)

🚗 *45mins from Pienza*

○ Buonconvento

Continue to medieval **San Quirico d'Orcia** to visit its lush Horti Leonini and sip a refreshing craft beer at Birrificio San Quirico (p119)

🚗 *15mins from Pienza*

Head to **Montalcino** for a glass or a few of its prized Brunello wine (p122)

🚗 *30mins from Pienza*

Torrenieri

○ Lama

Val d'Orcia

VAL D'ORCIA
Trip Builder

━━━ You don't need much to experience beautiful Val d'Orcia at its fullest – hit the roads twisting among its picturesque cypress-adorned hills and discover a culture shaped by nature and its seasons. Enjoy this Unesco World Heritage Site at a slow pace – one medieval town at the time – and you'll be rewarded by exceptional wine, food and views.

Break your journey in **Bagno Vignoni**, where thermal waters and relaxing spas await (p124)

🚗 *20mins from Pienza*

o Trequanda

o Montisi

Petroio o

o Castelmuzio

Fill up with truffle-based delicacies in the ancient settlement of **San Giovanni d'Asso** (p114)
🚗 30mins from Pienza

Stop in wonderful **Pienza** to admire its unique Renaissance architecture built under the order of Pope Pius II (p112)
🚗 1hr from Siena

Stop in **Montepulciano** to taste its Vino Nobile di Montepulciano (p121)
🚗 20mins from Pienza

Chianciano Terme ●

Take a sunset drive to **Monticchiello** for golden views and perfect photographs (p119)
🚗 15mins from Pienza

The Spa Towns

Sarteano o

Practicalities

BIM/GETTY IMAGES ©

ARRIVING

Air Pisa, Florence and Rome airports are all between 2 and 2½ hours from Val d'Orcia by car. Ryanair and British Airways also run some flights to Perugia, 1½ hours' drive away.

Train All towns in the Val d'Orcia area are located in the province of Siena, which is easily reached by train from Florence and Pisa. Other nearby stations are Buonconvento and Chiusi-Chianciano Terme.

HOW MUCH FOR A

Wine tasting
€30

Plate of *pici*
€10

White truffle
€2000/kg

GETTING AROUND

Car Driving is the best way to visit the Val d'Orcia, especially if you want to explore beyond urban centres. Major car rental companies operate in Siena.

Public transport From Siena, a 30-minute train ride takes you to Buonconvento, where you'll find bus 114 to Montalcino and bus 112 to San Quirico d'Orcia, Pienza and Montepulciano.

Bicycle The gentle hills and disparate villages make the Val d'Orcia perfect for exploring on two wheels. Cicloposse in Pienza offers bike and e-bike rentals, itineraries and guided tours.

WHEN TO GO

JAN–MAR
The weather is cold and unreliable, but if you're lucky, Val d'Orcia will be covered in snow.

APR–JUN
Ideal temperatures, colourful landscapes and open businesses. Best time to visit.

JUL–SEP
Fields turn golden as the climate gets warmer. The heat can be overwhelming.

OCT–DEC
Warm colours and cooler temperatures make early autumn a great time to visit.

EATING & DRINKING

Staying in an *agriturismo* (farm stay) means also getting to taste some of the freshest produce available in the region. Organic farms that offer hospitality will typically provide their own jams, olive oil, bread, cheese or wine during meals. *Pici* (pictured top) is Val d'Orcia's traditional pasta – thick, hand-rolled strings made of water and flour – best enjoyed with a *pecorino* sauce or *aglione,* the local variety of garlic, with a glass of Orcia, Montalcino or Montepulciano wine alongside.

Best Vino Nobile tasting
Cantina Ercolani (p122)

Must-try *pici*
Osteria di Porta al Cassero (p127)

CONNECT & FIND YOUR WAY

Wi-fi Most accommodation offers wi-fi, although it can be slow and patchy in the countryside.

Navigation The official tourism board of the Val d'Orcia provides a series of detailed maps you can download free of charge from the website visitvaldorcia.it.

UNESCO WORLD HERITAGE

The Val d'Orcia Park of Art, Nature and Culture is listed by Unesco as a cultural landscape. More information on the area can be found at parcodellavaldorcia.com.

WHERE TO STAY

All of the towns in the Val d'Orcia area retain their medieval feel. In the countryside, stunning landscapes and foodie experiences await.

Place	Pro/Con
Montalcino	Easy to explore both the Val d'Orcia and the Maremma between one wine tasting and the other.
Pienza	Surrounded by farm stays and increasingly used to international tourism; the perfect balance between nature and culture.
Montepulciano	The largest town in the region offers a lively atmosphere, great food options and a rich wine heritage.
Chianciano Terme	A resort town set in the countryside and based around natural thermal spas.
Agriturismi	Find farm-stay accommodation dotted around the countryside; away from the main towns but a great way to taste local food and be immersed in nature.

MONEY

By law all businesses in Italy have to accept cards but it's a good idea to always carry some cash when travelling in the countryside. American Express cards might be rejected at times.

16 Utopian **PIENZA**

ARCHITECTURE | HAMLET | WORLD HERITAGE SITE

Pienza is not simply another ancient *borgo* (hamlet). Of the many historic settlements found in Southern Tuscany, this town of 2000 or so residents stands out for its Renaissance roots – an architectural marvel designed in the 15th century to be the 'ideal city' nestled in the lush countryside of Unesco-listed Val d'Orcia.

KRISZTIAN JUHASZ/SHUTTERSTOCK ©

🗺 **How to**

Getting here Despite its fame, Pienza is not well connected by public transport. From Siena, take bus 57P to San Quirico d'Orcia, then bus 112 to Pienza. Consider going by car.

When to go Make the most of your Val d'Orcia trip by visiting in spring or autumn.

Tickets The Pienza Città di Luce Pass (€12) is valid for two days and includes entrance to Palazzo Piccolomini and its gardens, the crypt and Palazzo Borgia.

LAURA FACCHINI/SHUTTERSTOCK ©

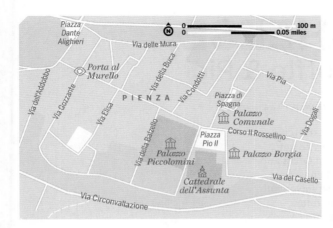

Top left Piazza Pio II and the Cattedrale dell'Assunta **Bottom left** Garden, Palazzo Piccolomini

Piccolomini's ideal city Pienza's origins are closely linked to the utopian vision of Enea Silvio Piccolomini, a humanist born in nearby Corsignano in 1405 who became pope in 1458 under the name of Pius II. Before 1459 – the year in which the new pope decided to build the ideal Renaissance city in the heart of the Val d'Orcia – the area occupied by Pienza today was virtually desolated. Architect Bernardo Rossellino, a student of Leon Battista Alberti, designed the urban plan from scratch following the neoclassical taste of the time, creating the grandiose papal residence that makes Pienza the pearl of the Renaissance we know today.

A unique *borgo* Unlike many other Tuscan hamlets built during Etruscan or medieval times, Pienza's character is defined by travertine facades, marble columns and imposing palaces – all built in only three years. Enter the town via Porta al Murello and you'll soon reach **Piazza Pio II**, where the white **Cattedrale dell'Assunta** is found near the marvellous **Palazzo Piccolomini**, the official papal residence, and its hidden Italian gardens facing Monte Amiata. Inside the cathedral you can admire panels by some of the most important Sienese painters of the time, including Lorenzo di Pietro, known as il Vecchietta, and Giovanni di Paolo. Without leaving the square you can also visit the Museo Diocesano inside **Palazzo Borgia**, the palace Pope Pius II donated to Cardinal Borgia which now hosts a permanent exhibition of rare medieval artworks in its 11 rooms.

Between Science & Faith

If you look down on the ground of Piazza Pio II, you'll notice that the square is composed of nine rectangles divided by travertine stripes. This design is not casual: twice a year the shadow of the Cattedrale dell'Assunta fills the rectangles exactly, making the church a giant sundial marking the spring and autumn equinoxes as (wrongly) indicated on the Julian calendar at the time. The switch to the Gregorian calendar in 1582 made it so that the phenomena no longer matches the astrological event. Today, the projection can be observed approximately 10 days after the spring equinox and 10 days before the autumn equinox.

17 CHEESE,
Truffle & Pici

LOCAL DELICACIES | FESTIVALS | TASTINGS

▬▬▬ The twisting roads stretching south from Siena are likely to get you hungry – luckily, Val d'Orcia and the neighbouring Crete Senesi area produce some of the most flavourful delicacies Tuscany has to offer. Whether it is San Giovanni D'Asso's truffles, Pienza's famed *pecorino* or the ever-present *pici,* the area's rich culinary culture will fuel your journey and delight your taste buds.

How to

When to go You'll easily find traditional specialities year-round, but for the best culinary experience visit in spring or autumn, when truffles are typically found.

Getting around Buses 112 and 119 connect Val d'Orcia's main centres, although driving is the best way to see the area.

Giant garlic Together with nearby Val di Chiana, Val d'Orcia grows a kind of garlic called *aglione*, known for its large cloves and sweet taste. Try it with *pici*.

Everything truffle The tiny hamlet of **San Giovanni d'Asso**, known to have existed since Etruscan times, sits just beyond Val d'Orcia's border in the Crete Senesi area, known for its clay-rich soil. There's more than clay to be found underground, however. The town is an important centre for truffles; depending on the season you might find white, marzuolo or scorzone truffle varieties. The **Mostra Mercato del Tartufo Bianco** takes place on the second and third weekends of November, while the **Festa del Tartufo Marzuolo** is held in March. Here is also the first Italian museum dedicated to the sought-after tuber, the **Museo del Tartufo**.

Top right *Pecorino*, Pienza
Bottom right *Pici* being made

MARAZE/SHUTTERSTOCK ©

PECORINO FRESCO
€ 12.80 al Kg

PECORINO STRACCHINO
€ 14.90

PECORINO SEMIFRESCO
€ 14.80 al Kg

SENIA EFFE/EYEEM/GETTY IMAGES ©

🍴 Don't Miss Pici

Thick and strictly hand-rolled, *pici* resembles spaghetti and are served in almost every restaurant in the area. In May the Crete Senesi hamlet of Casciano dei Bagni hosts the **Sagra dei Pici** (sagradeipici.it), a local celebration of the dish where plates brimming with sauce-soaked pasta are served to all in the town's main square.

Barrel-aged cheese When you stop in **Pienza**, make sure to taste the product the town is most proud of – its barrel-aged *pecorino*. A hard cheese made from sheep's milk, Pienza's *pecorino* is matured for at least 90 days in oak barriques which have often been used to age wine in the past. If you're in Pienza during the first week of September, don't miss the **Fiera del Cacio** and the fun **Palio del Cacio Fuso**, during which historical town districts compete by rolling wheels of cheese around a wooden spindle placed in the middle of the central square. At any other time of the year, you can still order a delicious tasting tray at **La Taverna del Pecorino** or at the **Enoteca Marusco e Maria**, where you'll be able to compare the different interpretations of this intense cheese.

VAL D'ORCIA'S
Foodie Highlights

01 Olive oil
Tuscan cooking is nothing without olive oil, and Val d'Orcia has no shortage of *frantoi* (oil mills) you can visit.

02 Truffles
White truffles grow especially around San Giovanni d'Asso, where you can also pay a visit to the Truffle Museum.

03 Aglione
The aptly named *aglione* – which means 'big garlic' – is sweeter than its smaller relative and becomes a tasty sauce for *pici*.

04 Snails
Chiocciole (snails) make a traditional dish in San Quirico, where restaurants serve them in a sauce of tomato, red wine and mortadella.

05 Red wines
Val d'Orcia's soil gives life to several of Tuscany's most prized wines, including DOC Orcia wines, Brunello di Montalcino and Vino Nobile di Montepulciano.

06 Pici
This hand-rolled pasta resembles very thick spaghetti and originates in Montalcino. It is often served with porcini mushrooms or a wild-boar *ragù*.

07 Chickpeas
Locally grown *ceci* (chickpeas) are often served with *verze* (Savoy cabbage) as a side dish.

08 Chestnuts
The lava dome of Monte Amiata is famed for *castagne* (chestnuts), which can be roasted or ground to a flour for pastas and breads.

09 Pecorino
Not to be confused with its namesakes from Rome and Sardinia, *pecorino toscano* is a hard sheep's milk cheese particular to Pienza.

10 Porcini mushrooms
The inhabitants of Vivo d'Orcia celebrate this nutty fungus alongside chestnuts at the annual Sagra del Fungo e della Castagna in October.

18 A Perfect Tuscan DRIVE

ROAD TRIP | LANDSCAPES | PHOTOGRAPHY

Few roads are as picturesque as those hugging Val d'Orcia's cypress-dotted hills. Come here in spring to see iconic Tuscan postcards come to life in bright green colours, or visit in early summer to see the fields of this Unesco-listed region turn golden.

JAROPIENZA/GETTY IMAGES ©

📷 Crete Senesi

As you drive through the Val d'Orcia you'll often cross into the neighbouring Crete Senesi – an area known for its grey hills produced by its clay-rich soil. To best experience this unique and unusual corner of Italy, drive through the spectacular landscape of the **Riserva Naturale Lucciola Bella**.

🗺 Trip Notes

How long If you start your trip from Siena, Pisa or Florence, take at least three days to explore Val d'Orcia and the bordering Crete Senesi area.

When to go In late July and August temperatures often rise above the bearable – it's best to visit before or after the summer.

Cycling Low levels of traffic makes the area great for cycling tours as well. Due to the hilly geography, electric bikes are becoming increasingly popular.

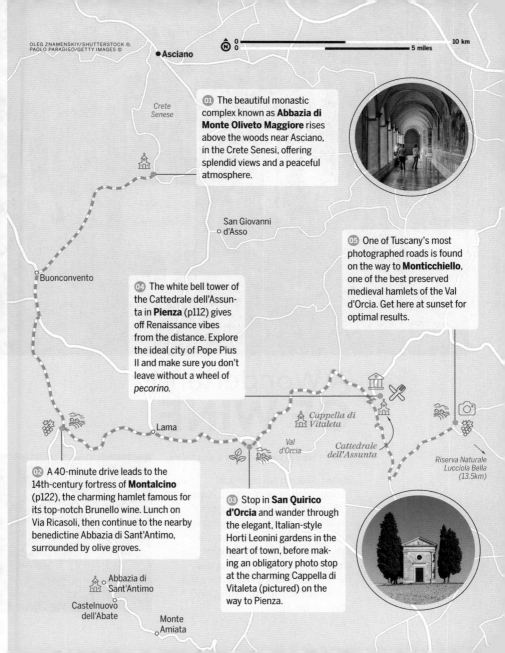

● **Asciano**

Crete Senese

01 The beautiful monastic complex known as **Abbazia di Monte Oliveto Maggiore** rises above the woods near Asciano, in the Crete Senesi, offering splendid views and a peaceful atmosphere.

San Giovanni
o d'Asso

05 One of Tuscany's most photographed roads is found on the way to **Monticchiello**, one of the best preserved medieval hamlets of the Val d'Orcia. Get here at sunset for optimal results.

▪ Buonconvento

04 The white bell tower of the Cattedrale dell'Assunta in **Pienza** (p112) gives off Renaissance vibes from the distance. Explore the ideal city of Pope Pius II and make sure you don't leave without a wheel of *pecorino*.

o Lama

Cappella di Vitaleta

Val d'Orcia

Cattedrale dell'Assunta

Riserva Naturale Lucciola Bella (13.5km)

02 A 40-minute drive leads to the 14th-century fortress of **Montalcino** (p122), the charming hamlet famous for its top-notch Brunello wine. Lunch on Via Ricasoli, then continue to the nearby benedictine Abbazia di Sant'Antimo, surrounded by olive groves.

03 Stop in **San Quirico d'Orcia** and wander through the elegant, Italian-style Horti Leonini gardens in the heart of town, before making an obligatory photo stop at the charming Cappella di Vitaleta (pictured) on the way to Pienza.

o Abbazia di Sant'Antimo

Castelnuovo
dell'Abate

Monte
o Amiata

0 — 10 km
0 — 5 miles

19 A Wonderland
OF WINE

WINE | MEDIEVAL TOWNS | SCENERY

Montepulciano and Montalcino have much in common – they produce two of Tuscany's greatest reds and are among Italy's most famous wine destinations. But despite their similarities, these charming medieval towns have their own distinct characters that are worth getting to know, one glass at the time.

How to

Drinking and driving
While the town centres can be reached by public transport, most wineries cannot. Italy's blood alcohol limit for drivers is 0.5gm per litre – not much. Join a guided tour or have a designated driver.

When to go Spring offers the best weather, but the weeks leading up to the harvest (late summer to early autumn) are great, as the grapes are ripe and still hanging from the vines, making the countryside landscapes particularly scenic.

Costs A wine tasting session typically starts from €15 to €25.

Montepulciano

An ancient *borgo* Located between Val d'Orcia and Val di Chiana, Montepulciano is a fascinating *borgo* believed to have existed since Etruscan times. Flourishing as an important strategic centre under the Medici's rule in the 16th century, the city is best known for its **Vino Nobile di Montepulciano**, the legendary pour whose production is documented since 789. To acquire its 'noble' status, Montepulciano's signature vino has to be made with at least 70% Sangiovese grapes and has to be aged for a minimum of two years, of which at least one should be in wood. Make sure not to confuse Montepulciano's Vino Nobile with the Montepulciano d'Abruzzo wine – a blasphemous comparison that will cause locals more pain than the machinery found at the city's Torture Museum.

Did Someone Say Beer?

If you're yearning for some hops, head to Montepulciano's first brewpub, **Miglio Verde**, where brews by the Birrificio di Montepulciano are served, or the excellent **Birrificio l'Olmaia** nearby. If you're in San Quirico stop at the **Birrificio San Quirico**.

Above left Brunello di Montalcino (p122) **Above right** Montalcino
Left Vineyard, Montepulciano

Noble tastings Plenty of wineries are scattered around Montepulciano, offering the opportunity to taste their Vino Nobile and other varieties of local wine. A good place to start is the **Cantina Ercolani**, in the town centre, which features an Underground City museum showing barrel-filled ancient cellars expanding below historic palaces. Similarly, the **Cantina de' Ricci** will allow you to explore their beautiful, subterranean exposed-brick cellars and gain fascinating insight into the history and production of the wine. After the city explorations, head out to the **Avignonesi** winery, where next to their biodynamic Vino Nobile you'll be able to taste their sweet, Occhio di Pernice Vin Santo – a 'holy' wine aged for 10 years, whose origins are rooted in the Renaissance.

Montalcino

The town and its Brunello Montalcino's signature wine has a much more recent history

🍷 Bravìo delle Botti

Each year, on the last Sunday of August, Montepulciano celebrates its patron St John the Baptist with a sporting event unlike any other, which follows a parade in the city's historic centre. The Bravìo delle Botti is a challenge that sees the eight *contrade* (districts) of the town compete by rolling wine barrels weighing up to 80kg on an uphill street leading to Piazza Grande, the city's main square, wearing traditional costumes. The efforts of the winners are rewarded with the *bravìo*, a painted cloth carrying the image of St John.

Crete
Senese

Avignonesi

San Giovanni
d'Asso

Petrignano

Buonconvento

Casato
Prime
Donne

Tempio del
Brunello

Cantina
Ercolani

Val
d'Orcia

Pienza

Montepulciano
Cantina de' Ricci

Montalcino

San Quirico d'Orcia

Monticchiello

Val di
Chiana

Lago di
Chiusi

NostraVita

Enoteca la Fortezza
di Montalcino

Castelnuovo
dell'Abate

Castiglione
d'Orca

Chiusi

Ciacci
Piccolomini
D'Aragona

Monte Amiata

Sarteano

0   10 km
0   5 miles

Left Bravio delle Botti, Montepulciano
Below Cantina Ercolani, Montepulciano

than its Montepulciano counterpart. The name 'Brunello' – now one the world's most sought-after labels – was invented in the late 1800s by the Biondi Santi family, who wanted to diversify their high-quality Sangiovese production. To maintain the high standard, strict rules apply to producers today – including a minimum of two years of ageing in oak and a five-year delay between the harvest and the market release. You can learn all about the wine in the newly opened **Tempio del Brunello**, an interactive museum located in Montalcino's Sant'Agostino complex.

Brunello tastings Montalcino's tiny town centre has many *enoteche* (wine bars) lining up one after the other, including the **Enoteca la Fortezza di Montalcino**, found inside the fortress. Here you can learn about the different facets of local wine production, before heading to the nearby countryside to visit one of the many wineries, such as the art-filled, family-run **NostraVita** or the historic **Ciacci Piccolomini D'Aragona** winery, still operating in a majestic 17th-century palace in Castelnuovo dell'Abate. If you're still thirsty, continue for a vertical tasting of six vintages of Brunello di Montalcino at the **Casato Prime Donne**, the first Italian winery run exclusively by women, founded by local entrepreneur Donatella Cinelli Colombini.

20 The Valley's Hot **SPRINGS**

HOT SPRINGS | NATURE | OUTDOORS

The Val d'Orcia does self-care like nowhere else in Italy. Face masks and bubble baths are for amateurs: here wellness rituals aren't an Instagram performance but a way of life tied to thermal baths, long-lost civilisations, medieval pilgrimage roads and sulphur-rich waters. Make like the Etruscans and Romans and indulge in a healing dip in the area's many hot springs.

ESSEVU/SHUTTERSTOCK ©

📍 **How to**

Getting around A car is a must in this area. Bagno Vignoni is about an hour south of Siena if you follow the Via Cassia SR2. Bagni San Filippo is around half an hour from the Tuscany–Lazio border, on the eastern edge of Monte Amiata.

When to go February to April is generally less crowded if you're really looking to relax in peace.

Get prepared Take a towel with you when heading to the hot springs – don't expect the amenities of the in-town spa facilities!

FABIO LAMANNA/SHUTTERSTOCK ©

Etruscans and Romans relied on hot springs for bathing and for their mystical-medicinal properties. Modern travellers on the hunt for restorative experiences have followed suit.

Bagno Vignoni Just off a stretch of the Via Francigena (p210), the medieval pilgrimage road between Canterbury and Rome, the central square in this celeb-favoured town features a 49m-length pool filled with hot springs water. Although you can't take a dip in the photogenic waters, you can walk beyond the square, passing the former mills and heading toward the **Parco dei Mulini**, which offers free access to the hot springs.

Bagni San Filippo Further south at the foot of Monte Amiata, Bagni San Filippo borders on seductive: its travertine rock and gently rippling waterfalls instantly soothe before you've even dipped your toes in. The town is home to numerous hotels and spa complexes, but the best option is the free-entry **Terme San Filippo**, outdoor hot springs set in the woods just outside town. Follow the path toward the impressive, calciferous **Balena Bianca** (White Whale) waterfall, which often shape-shifts in terms of water flow and rock colours.

Chianciano Terme Federico Fellini shot some key scenes from his classic 8½ in this resort town. A highlight here are the **Piscine Termali Theia**, named for an Etruscan mythological figure and fed by the Sillene thermal spring. If you're a little tired of just unwinding – though why would you be? – the nearby **Parco Fucoli** holds the Palamontepeschi, a 990-seat venue offering live entertainment and activities.

Top left Bagno Vignoni
Bottom left Balena Bianca waterfall, Bagni San Filippo

San Casciano dei Bagni

It's technically south of the Val d'Orcia, but this sleepy resort town in what was once Etruria bears a mention. A border-town at the crux of Lazio, Tuscany and Umbria, San Casciano dei Bagni is home to 42 thermal springs and has wooed in famous figures dating back to Emperor Augustus. There's free entrance to the **Bagno Bossolo** and **Bagno Grande**, which can both be reached from the main town square.

Listings

BEST OF THE REST

 ## Picturesque Nature, Scenic Roads & Photo Ops

Cypress Avenue Poggio Covili

The Agriturismo Poggio Covili features one of the most photogenic roads in all of the Val d'Orcia. Stop for a self-made postcard or book a room to immerse yourself in the landscape.

Cipressi di San Quirico d'Orcia

Perhaps the most photographed group of trees in Italy, this ring of cypresses emerges gloriously from an empty field by the SR2 road that connects San Quirico d'Orcia with Torrenieri.

Bosco della Ragnaia

In the 1990s, American artist Sheppard Craige created a garden-sculpture park near San Giovanni d'Asso, where the natural elements become philosophical symbols embedded in the landscape.

Giardino La Foce

Designed by British landscape architect Cecil Pinsent, the garden of Villa La Foce is one of Tuscany's most refined. Symmetrical plant sculptures are surrounded by wisterias, cypresses and a travertine staircase, with magnificent views of Val d'Orcia and the Monte Amiata.

Quercia delle Checche

This 300-year-old oak tree near the Lucciola Bella Nature Reserve is a protected living monument, with a height of 22m and nearly 20m in diameter.

 ## Festivals & Events

Incontri in Terra di Siena

Theatres, courtyards and piazzas open for a series of classical music events at the end of July organised by the owners of Villa La Foce. Check the full programme at itslafoce.org.

Val d'Orcia Art Festival

Local and international artists gather in Radicofani in September for a series of workshops and exhibitions showcasing classical and contemporary crafts. More info at valdorciaartfestival.it.

Jazz & Wine in Montalcino

In July Montalcino's fortress becomes a scenic open-air theatre hosting international jazz and blues acts. Full programme at jazzandwinemontalcino.it.

Orcia Wine Festival

San Quirico d'Orcia hosts a festival dedicated to the Orcia wine each April, when producers and enthusiasts gather to taste, discuss and celebrate the different varieties of this local wine.

Architecture & Historic Sites

Castello di Spedaletto

A grandiose 12th-century fortification located near Pienza, originally belonging to Siena's Santa Maria della Scala Hospital (p103), one of the oldest in Europe.

Museo della Mezzadria Senese

In charming Buonconvento, this museum is entirely dedicated to documenting how the *mezzadria* (sharecropping) system functioned in rural areas until the 1970s, dictating the lifestyles of the people living in the Tuscan countryside.

Fortezza di Radicofani

At the top of a 900m-tall rock formation, the thousand-year-old Radicofani Castle was built as a defensive structure to oversee the traffic on the nearby Via Cassia, which connected Florence to Rome.

Rocca d'Orcia

An imposing tower built in the 11th century by the powerful Aldobrandeschi family that used to rule over Southern Tuscany rises tall above Castiglione d'Orcia. Views to the surrounding valley are spectacular.

Restaurants & More Wine

Dopolavoro La Foce   €€

An ideal refuge after a day spent exploring. Sit down to coffee and gourmet dishes in a bright, welcoming space set in a historic building near Pienza.

Latte di Luna   €€

In Pienza's charming historic centre, this little restaurant has become a local institution thanks to its changing menu of typical dishes made with fresh ingredients.

Osteria di Porta al Cassero   €€

Pici, wild boar, cured meats and great wine – this family-run restaurant in the heart of Montalcino has made simplicity its trademark, honouring the territory with many delicious all-time classics.

Trattoria Toscana al Vecchio Forno   €€

Genuine Tuscan cuisine served in a warm setting surrounded by greenery in San Quirico d'Orcia. Book a table in the garden, if weather allows.

Fonte alla Vena   €€

Refined regional classics ranging from *panzanella* (Tuscan chopped salad) to Florentine steak are served on the terrace of a beautiful stone building near San Quirico d'Orcia's main street.

Fattoria dei Barbi

Run by the Colombini family since the 18th century, this winery is a Montalcino institution, producing Brunello for over a century.

Poggio Antico

Set on Montalcino's highest hill, Poggio Antico is a beautiful property surrounded by cypresses, overlooking the Tyrrhenian Sea.

Agriturismo Stays

Agriturismo Le Macchie

A nature-immersed stay near Pienza in a 17th-century building nestled in the rolling hills. Base yourself here and explore the valley with the bikes available for rent.

Terra Antica

Surrounded by vineyards and olive groves, Montepulciano's luxurious Terra Antica combines traditional, organic food with modern amenities such as an outdoor gym and a yoga area.

Rosewood Castiglion del Bosco

This idyllic, luxurious resort owned by the Ferragamo family in the heart of Val d'Orcia was named best in Europe by *Travel + Leisure* in 2022.

 Scan to find more things to do in Val d'Orcia online

VAL D'ORCIA REVIEWS

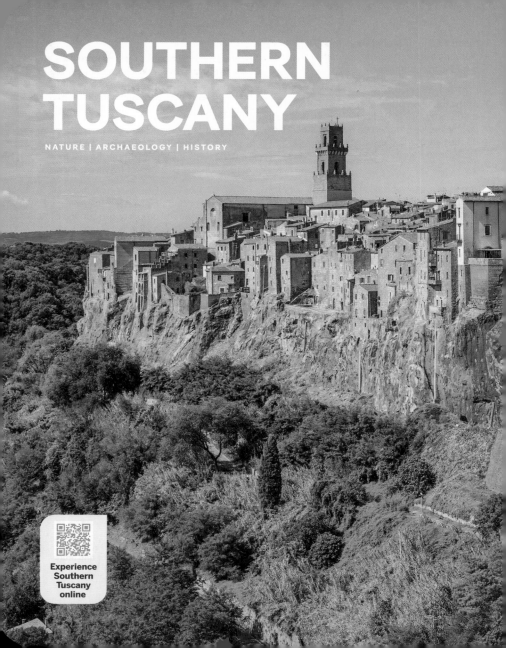

SOUTHERN TUSCANY

NATURE | ARCHAEOLOGY | HISTORY

Experience
Southern
Tuscany
online

Visit historic **Massa Marittima** for some culture away from the crowds (p144)
🚗 1½hrs from Siena

Monterotondo Marittimo

Montebamboli ○   ○ Pian di Mucini

Tatti ○

Baratti ○   CENTRAL COAST   Montemassi ○

Dive into the turquoise waters of the not-so-secret **Cala Violina** (p149)
🚗 40mins from Piombino

Piombino ○   *Golfo di Follonica*

Bagno di ○ Gavorrano
○ Gavorrano
○ Follonica   ○ Fontino
Montepescali ○

Bandite di Scarlino   🏢 Braccagni ○

After a hike, take a beach break at the **Spiaggia delle Rocchette**, near Castiglione della Pescaia (p150)
🚗 35mins from Grosseto

Elba

○ Punta Ala

Castiglione della Pescaia

Marina di ○ Grosseto

SOUTHERN TUSCANY
Trip Builder

Immerse yourself in the bird-brimming nature of the **Parco Regionale della Maremma** (p134)
🚗 20mins from Grosseto

Marina di Alberese ○

▬▬▬▬ Despite being one of Tuscany's lesser-visited regions, the geographical area known as Maremma – which covers much of Southern Tuscany – combines an invaluable Etruscan heritage with wild nature overflowing with unique flora and fauna. A tour of the south will take you from mesmerising beach coves to archaeological sites and ancient castles nestled on towering rock formations, and along roads cutting between seemingly endless Sangiovese vineyards.

Go for some off-season snorkelling in the blue waters of **Cala del Gesso**, Monte Argentario (p151)
🚗 45mins from Grosseto

Giglio

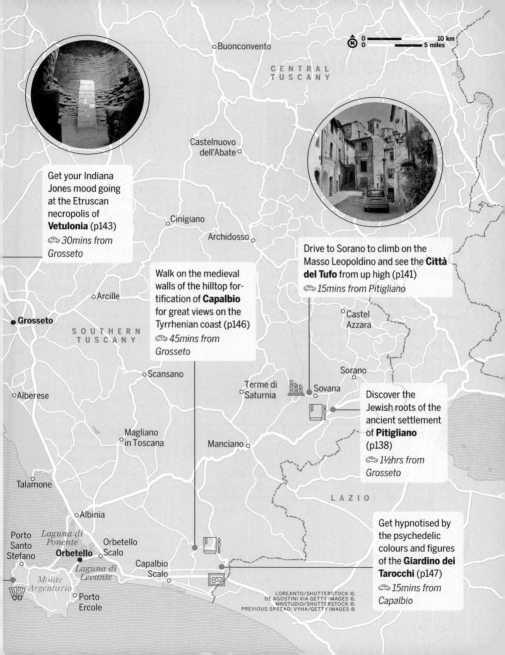

Buonconvento

CENTRAL TUSCANY

0 — 10 km
0 — 5 miles

Castelnuovo dell'Abate

Get your Indiana Jones mood going at the Etruscan necropolis of **Vetulonia** (p143)
🚗 *30mins from Grosseto*

Cinigiano

Archidosso

Walk on the medieval walls of the hilltop fortification of **Capalbio** for great views on the Tyrrhenian coast (p146)
🚗 *45mins from Grosseto*

Drive to Sorano to climb on the Masso Leopoldino and see the **Città del Tufo** from up high (p141)
🚗 *15mins from Pitigliano*

Arcille

Grosseto

SOUTHERN TUSCANY

Castel Azzara

Scansano

Terme di Saturnia

Sovana

Sorano

Alberese

Discover the Jewish roots of the ancient settlement of **Pitigliano** (p138)
🚗 *1½hrs from Grosseto*

Magliano in Toscana

Manciano

LAZIO

Talamone

Albinia

Porto Santo Stefano

Laguna di Ponente

Orbetello Scalo

Orbetello

Laguna di Levante

Capalbio Scalo

Get hypnotised by the psychedelic colours and figures of the **Giardino dei Tarocchi** (p147)
🚗 *15mins from Capalbio*

Monte Argentario

Porto Ercole

LOREANTO/SHUTTERSTOCK ©,
DE AGOSTINI VIA GETTY IMAGES ©,
MNSTUDIO/SHUTTERSTOCK ©,
PREVIOUS SPREAD: VYHA/GETTY IMAGES ©

Practicalities

YURI TURKOV/SHUTTERSTOCK ©

ARRIVING

Air Much of Southern Tuscany is closer to Rome's airports (Fiumicino pictured) than it is to Florence or Pisa. Consider all three when booking.

Train Grosseto is Maremma's main city and transport hub, easily reached from Pisa and Siena in approximately 1½ hours.

Bus From Florence, the fastest way to get to Grosseto is by bus. Tiemme bus 50G runs between the two cities on weekdays in just over two hours. Check schedules at tiemmespa.it.

HOW MUCH FOR A

Gelato scoop
€2.50

Wine tasting
€25

Beach umbrella
€30 per day

GETTING AROUND

Driving A car is pretty much the only way to get around, especially if time is limited. Maremma is a vast region and while buses do connect rural towns they are few and far between. The E80 motorway cuts through all of Maremma, providing the quickest way to get from A to B in the region. Major car-hire companies operate in Grosseto, although it's probably easier and more time efficient to rent your vehicle at Pisa's airport and start your road trip from there.

Cycling While the interior is hilly, the western side of Maremma is mostly flat making it suitable for short- and long-distance cycling thanks to an extensive network of dedicated paths, inside and outside the nature reserve. Avoid the peak summer season as the heat gets overwhelming. Check out piste-ciclabili.com/provincia-grosseto for detailed information on the available routes.

WHEN TO GO

JAN–MAR
Unpredictable weather; most tourist infrastructure goes into hibernation.

APR–JUN
The parks are in full bloom and the beaches are still empty. Best time to explore.

JUL–SEP
Likely too hot to hike, but great for road trips, canoeing, swimming and wine tasting.

OCT–DEC
Nature changes colours as days get shorter; early autumn is still optimal for exploring.

EATING & DRINKING

While its long coastline might suggest a primary spot for seafood in the local cuisine, Maremma is most proud of it hearty meat dishes such as the *tortelli maremmani al ragù* (spinach-stuffed ravioli covered in *ragù*) or the *pappardelle alla lepre* (long, flat pasta in hare sauce). Most local specialities, such as *acquacotta* (literally 'cooked water', a Tuscan broth soup; pictured bottom), originate in the rural tradition best represented by the *butteri,* the Maremmese cowboys still active in the region. But food isn't all the area has to offer – flagship wine Morellino di Scansano (pictured top) is the obligatory pairing to your journey.

Must-try *pappardelle al cinghiale*
Taverna del Vecchio Borgo (p153)

Best Morellino di Scansano tasting
Roccapesta (p147)

CONNECT & FIND YOUR WAY

Wi-fi The majority of hotels, cafes and restaurants offer free wi-fi, but it's best to buy your own prepaid SIM card if you need an internet connection to navigate while driving. Activation costs about €20 (depending on the service provider).

Parking Street-side parking spaces are typically marked either by blue or white lines. In the first case it means you have to pay to park, in the latter it's free.

BOOK AHEAD

Make sure to book tours to visit the Parco Regionale della Maremma (p134) at least a day in advance. Between mid-June and mid-September a certified guide is required due to the high risk of fires.

WHERE TO STAY

Covering a quarter of Tuscany, Maremma offers accommodation options for any taste. Choose between bucolic countryside stays, beachside residences just steps from the sand or city hotels.

Town	Pro/Con
Grosseto	The largest city and main transport hub; built around Piazza Dante, with easy access to the nearby nature reserve and archaeological areas.
Massa Marittima	Culture, good food, relaxed atmosphere in Alta Maremma.
Pitigliano	The best base to explore Città del Tufo and the tiny hamlets in its surroundings.
Scansano	Not much happening in the town itself, but there are many welcoming farmstays in the surrounding countryside.
Castiglione della Pescaia	Family-friendly beach town surrounded by nature; comes alive in July and August.
Monte Argentario	One of the most prized beach destinations in mainland Tuscany; prices skyrocket in summer.

MONEY

While shops are required by law to accept card payments, not all do. It's best to carry some cash. Some shop owners will also frown upon making small payments with a card, but you are allowed to do so.

21 Untamed
MAREMMA

NATURE | OUTDOORS | HIKING

The Uccellina Mountains slope down to the Tyrrhenian Sea forming Tuscany's first regional park – a 9000-hectare ecosystem where Mediterranean forests and sand dunes surround abandoned medieval watchtowers and ancient abbeys. Explore the trails on foot or by mountain bike in pristine woods teeming with wildlife.

Above Parco Regionale della Maremma **Right** Abbazia di San Rabano

📷 How to

Getting here Enter Parco Regionale della Maremma via the towns of Alberese, in the northeast, or Talamone, in the south, both reachable on the SS1 Aurelia motorway.

Getting around The park is open year-round. Tickets (from €10) and trail maps can be bought at the **Alberese Visitor Centre** (Via Bersagliere 7/9) or online at parco-maremma.it.

Guided tours Due to the high risk of forest fires, entrance to the park is allowed only with a certified guide during summer months (15 June to 15 September).

Hiking & Cycling Trails

Twelve official hiking routes and eight cycling paths depart from the park's entry points, allowing you to discover the different facets of this diverse nature reserve based on your level of fitness and interests. From the easy A3 Caves circular trail, stretching south from the Casetta dei Pinottolai building and running for nearly 10km through thick woods and a series of natural rock cavities, to the more challenging C1 route leading to the immaculate Salto del Cervo beach, there is something for everyone here. Take your time to explore and make sure to leave no trace behind.

One of the most popular trails is the 16km A1 route, which will take you in the heart of the Uccellina Mountains to see the striking remains of the **Abbazia di San Rabano**, built by Benedictine monks between the 11th and 12th centuries and abandoned in the 16th century. Surrounded by thick woods, the soaring stone structure is a spectacle worth every effort. Near the abbey, you'll also find the 14th-century **Uccellina tower**, one of the many defence structures of this kind built on the coast to keep an eye on enemies approaching from the nearby sea.

The full, circular trek takes approximately seven hours to complete (so it's best to set off early); a shorter, 8km route marked as A1-B going from Alberese to the abbey and back can be done if you are short on time or energy.

Birdwatching on the Water

The proximity to mountains, rivers and sea creates the perfect conditions for a vast number of animals to live within the park's borders. Wild boars, deer, foxes and wild cats live side by side with over 270 species of birds – meaning that once you enter you'll be a birdwatcher whether you like it or not. Ospreys, barn owls, peregrine falcons and green woodpeckers are just some of the

Maremma's Cowboys

Part of the Parco Regionale della Maremma overlaps with one of Europe's largest organic farms, the **Tenuta di Alberese**. The estate, now owned by Tuscany's local government, extends for over 4000 hectares and keeps alive the tradition of the *butteri,* the cowboys who, generation after generation, continue to herd animals – especially the long-horned Maremmana cows – over vast areas of land from the back of their horses. Today over 500 Maremmana cows are left to roam free within the park's premises under the attentive eye of the last remaining *butteri.* Learn more at alberese.com.

Riserva Naturale Diaccia Botrona

This 1300-hectare nature reserve, 20km west of Grosseto, is another birdwatchers' paradise in Maremma. Flamingos, wild geese, great white egrets and cranes have made what's left of the now-drained Lake Prile home.

many species you might notice as you roam Maremma's wetlands. For the best chance to spot birds, join a canoe tour with a certified guide on the Ombrone river at sunrise when the forests awaken. Prices start at €35; book ahead via parco-maremma.it.

Marina di Alberese

The Parco Regionale della Maremma isn't just for the hyperactive. Marina di Alberese offers a pleasant respite from forest hikes with its fine sands stretching for 4km between pine trees and deep-blue waters. Cycle the 8km path from Alberese or drive to the nearby parking space, then walk down the coast to find a quiet spot away from the more crowded area by the entrance. About 2km south from the parking area there's a nudist beach. Bring your own water and food.

Left *Butteri* **Top** Egret, Riserva Naturale Diaccia Botrona
Above Marina di Alberese

The Little Jerusalem

A SHORT HISTORY OF PITIGLIANO'S JEWISH COMMUNITY

How a small hilltop settlement became a refuge for persecuted Jewish people – and how the community all but vanished in the centuries afterwards.

SAGA PHOTO AND VIDEO/SHUTTERSTOCK ©

As you walk down Via Zuccarelli in the town of Pitigliano, you might notice a sign with Gothic lettering placed above a stone arch pointing to the 'Piccola Gerusalemme' (Little Jerusalem). Follow the arrows and you'll soon come across the only functioning synagogue still active in Southern Tuscany – an unassuming building carrying forward the tradition of the small Jewish community that lived in the area for nearly five centuries.

The origins of the Jewish community of Pitigliano can be traced back to a papal bull released on July 1555 by Pope Paul IV, which established the first ghetto in Rome after claiming that coexistence between Christians and Jews was 'absurd and utterly inconvenient' since Jews 'through their own fault were condemned by God to eternal slavery'. The decree placed harsh limitations on the rights of Jewish people living in Rome: all members of the Jewish community were obliged to live within walled quarters that were locked at night and to wear an identifying badge, and they were forbidden to own any property. In 1570, similar laws were introduced in Tuscany by Grand Duke Cosimo I of the Medici family, who ordered the construction of Florence's ghetto near today's Piazza della Repubblica.

Many decided to flee the Papal State as a result. At the time, the remote hilltop settlement of Pitigliano was an independent county, a fief of the Orsini family landlocked between the Papal State and the Grand Duchy of Tuscany. The refugees found a place to live and work in peace on the volcanic tuff rock formations of the Maremmese countryside. The period of tranquillity, however, was short-lived: in 1604 the Orsini ceded control of the Pitigliano county to the Medici, who began heavily taxing Jewish-owned businesses

Above left Street, Pitigliano **Middle** Kosher wine cellar **Right** Synagogue

first and, later, setting up ghettos in Pitigliano and Sorano, just as they had done three decades earlier in the capital.

Over a century would have to pass for Pitigliano's Jewish community to gain back its freedom. Following the decline of the Medici in 1737, the Jewish population began flourishing, reaching its peak at the turn of the century when it made up approximately 12% of Pitigliano's 2400 residents. With the unification of Italy in 1861, many Jewish people could finally move to larger cities in search of better opportunities, but the final blow to the community in Pitigliano arrived with the introduction of the 1938 racial laws by Benito Mussolini's fascist government. At the time only 70 Jewish people were registered in Pitigliano – and fewer than half would survive the war; those who survived were assisted by local Christian families who provided protection in the countryside. Mussolini's racial laws would ultimately lead – through deportations and forced emigration – to a decline in the Jewish population in Italy by nearly 50%.

> In 1938 only 70 Jewish people were registered in Pitigliano – and fewer than half would survive the war.

Today only a handful of members of the once-thriving Jewish community remain in Pitigliano. La Piccola Gerusalemme (lapiccolagerusalemme.it) organisation takes care of maintaining the local kosher wine cellar, the bakery and the Jewish cemetery found near the 16th-century synagogue, renovated in 1995 after collapsing in the 1960. A museum of Jewish culture has been set up showcasing the history of the community through a collection of preserved artefacts.

✂️ Lo Sfratto

The dish that best represents the blending of Jewish and Maremmese traditions is perhaps a cake known as *lo sfratto* (the eviction) – an icon of Pitigliano's gastronomy made by filling a thin, cylindrical pastry shell with honey, chopped walnuts, nutmeg and aniseed. The tube shape is meant to be a reference to the sticks used by the Medici's military force to evict Jewish people from their houses when the ghettos were instituted in the early 17th century. Try it in bakeries such as **Forno del Ghetto** (Via Zuccarelli 167).

22

A Città del Tufo
ROAD TRIP

DRIVING TOUR | ARCHAEOLOGY | GEOLOGY

▬▬▬ Built on towering volcanic rock formations, the towns of Pitigliano, Sovana, Sorano and part of Castell'Azzara form the area known as the Città del Tufo (City of Tuff), where ancient Etruscan settlements and natural landscapes collide to form one of the most fascinating corners of Tuscany.

REDA&CO/UNIVERSAL IMAGES GROUP VIA GETTY IMAGES ©

🗺️ Trip Notes

Getting around From Siena, head south on the SR2 motorway for approximately 1½ hours, then turn right on the SP20 to reach Castell'Azzara.

Parco Archeologico Città del Tufo The 60-hectare archaeological park consists of three areas: the necropolis of Sovana, San Rocco (near Sorano) and Vitozza. Tickets cost €5.

Vie Cave There are 15 Etruscan *'vie cave'*, trench-like paths dating back to the 6th century BCE, dug up to 20m deep into the tuff rock. The Via Cava di San Giuseppe and the Via Cava di Fratenuti near Pitigliano are impressive.

♨️ Saturnia's Baths

On your way back to Grosseto or Siena, take a break at the public baths of Saturnia, where sulphurous waters run at a constant 37°C. Dive into one of the free pools, such as the hot springs known as Cascate del Mulino, known since Etruscan times for their health properties.

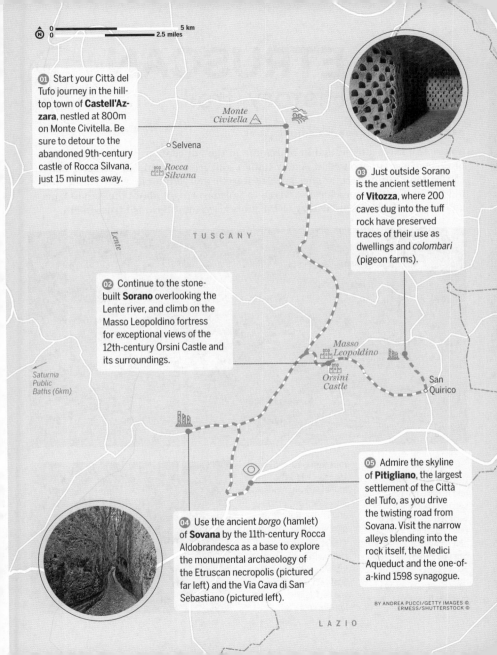

0 —————————— **5 km**
0 —————————— **2.5 miles**

01 Start your Città del Tufo journey in the hill-top town of **Castell'Azzara**, nestled at 800m on Monte Civitella. Be sure to detour to the abandoned 9th-century castle of Rocca Silvana, just 15 minutes away.

Monte Civitella ▲

○ Selvena

⌂ *Rocca Silvana*

Lente

TUSCANY

03 Just outside Sorano is the ancient settlement of **Vitozza**, where 200 caves dug into the tuff rock have preserved traces of their use as dwellings and *colombari* (pigeon farms).

02 Continue to the stone-built **Sorano** overlooking the Lente river, and climb on the Masso Leopoldino fortress for exceptional views of the 12th-century Orsini Castle and its surroundings.

Saturnia Public Baths (6km)

Masso Leopoldino

Orsini Castle

San ○ Quirico

05 Admire the skyline of **Pitigliano**, the largest settlement of the Città del Tufo, as you drive the twisting road from Sovana. Visit the narrow alleys blending into the rock itself, the Medici Aqueduct and the one-of-a-kind 1598 synagogue.

04 Use the ancient *borgo* (hamlet) of **Sovana** by the 11th-century Rocca Aldobrandesca as a base to explore the monumental archaeology of the Etruscan necropolis (pictured far left) and the Via Cava di San Sebastiano (pictured left).

BY ANDREA PUCCI/GETTY IMAGES ©,
ERMESS/SHUTTERSTOCK ©

LAZIO

23 ETRUSCAN
History Trail

ARCHAEOLOGY | HISTORY | ARCHITECTURE

The Etruscans settled in Maremma in the 7th century BCE and built some of the earliest cities on what is now Italian soil. Traces of this ancient civilisation can be found in important sites such as Roselle and Vetulonia, where millennia-old urban constructions have survived to this day. Forget about the Renaissance and step further back in history to the glorious yet mysterious Etruscan era.

PAOLO TROVO/GETTY IMAGES ©

🗺 How to

Getting here Vetulonia and Roselle are two separate parks north of Grosseto. Both can be reached by car in under half an hour. Both areas can be visited in a day.

Opening times Vetulonia has rather confusing opening times: the

museum is closed on Monday, while the tombs of Pietrera and Diavolino are closed on Tuesday and Friday. Roselle is closed on Monday.

Tickets Entry to the Isidoro Falchi Archaeological Museum in Vetulonia costs €5, while access to the park is free. Visiting Roselle costs €4.

GIULIO ANDREINI/UCG/UNIVERSAL IMAGES GROUP VIA GETTY IMAGES ©

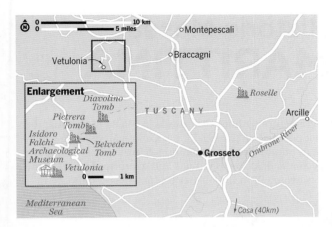

Top left Etruscan ruins, Roselle
Bottom left Exhibit, Isidoro Falchi Archaeological Museum, Vetulonia

Vetulonia For centuries, Vetulonia was a mythological Etruscan city known only through Roman texts which described it as a powerful commercial centre in the heart of Tuscany. Things changed in the 1840s, when a statue portraying three Etruscan deities with references to the lost civilisation of Vetulonia was uncovered near Cerveteri, Lazio, kickstarting a new stage of excavations. The city was finally rediscovered in the late 1880s and today is one of the most important archaeological parks in the region. Walk along the Via dei Sepolcri to visit the monumental **Belvedere**, **Pietrera** and **Diavolino Tombs**, three of the most impressive examples of Etruscan sculpture dating back to the 7th century BCE. Include a stop in the nearby **Archaeological Museum** dedicated to Italian archaeologist Isidoro Falchi to put the symbology into context and check out dozens of Etruscan artefacts that have emerged throughout the years.

Roselle The strategic position of Roselle (Rusellae) allowed Etruscan settlers to control the surrounding plains from above and access the sea via the Prile Lake (now Riserva Naturale Diaccia Botrona; p137), creating the perfect military and economic conditions for the city to flourish. The Romans took control of Roselle in 294 BCE. While Etruscan-era monuments are no longer visible, the urban plan remains intact inside the imposing stone walls, allowing you to picture where people lived and worked before the city was abandoned in 1138 after Pope Innocent XI transferred his diocese from Roselle to Grosseto.

The Ancient City of Cosa

In the 3rd century BCE, the Romans began conquering many territories in Maremma, building their own infrastructure on the foundations of former Etruscan cities. The archaeological park of Cosa, near Ansedonia, became a Roman colony in 273 BCE. The remains of public and private buildings are still visible to this day, with a clear division between the Arce, the temple where religious functions were performed (offering great views on the Argentario), and the forum, the heart of political life. It's open Friday, Saturday and Sunday.

Historic Massa
MARITTIMA

ART | HISTORY | CITY TOUR

Enjoy wonderful architecture without the crowds in Massa Marittima, the Alta Maremma hilltop town perched on the side of the Colline Metallifere which experienced its golden age as an independent commune between 1225 and 1337, before being conquered by Siena. Skip the long lines and overpriced gelati of the major art cities and immerse yourself in the medieval atmosphere found here.

MILOSK50/SHUTTERSTOCK ©

🗺 How to

Getting here The closest train station is in Follonica, 20km west. From there take bus 37F for 30 minutes. Check the schedule at at-bus.it.

Tickets A combined ticket including access to four museums and the Torre del Candeliere viewpoint is available for €15.

Top tip Lunch on delicious *tortelli alla maremmana* (pasta pockets filled with spinach and ricotta) in one of the local restaurants showing the Slow Food badge, such as **Le Fate Briache** (Corso A Diaz 3).

ORIETTA GASPARI/GETTY IMAGES ©

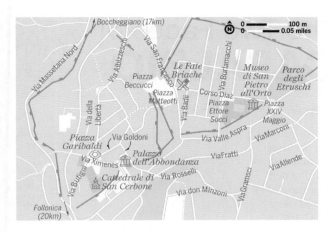

Top left Cattedrale di San Cerbone
Bottom left *Albero della Fecondità*, Palazzo dell'Abbondanza

A Romanesque-Gothic cathedral Start your visit in Piazza Garibaldi, the main square of Massa Vecchia (Old Massa) where the beautiful **Cattedrale di San Cerbone**, started in the 11th century and completed nearly 300 years later, combines Romanesque and Gothic elements. Get closer to admire Giovanni Pisano's sculptures of a kneeling man, a horse and a griffin holding the facade's columns, then enter to see sculptor Giroldo da Como's intricately carved *Baptismal Font* (1267), Duccio di Buoninsegna's painting *Madonna delle Grazie* (1318) and Goro di Gregorio's *Arca di San Cerbone* (1324), telling the story of Massa Marittima's patron saint.

Many of the magnificent sculptures by Giovanni Pisano that once embellished the Cattedrale di San Cerbone's facade have now been moved to the little **Museo di San Pietro all'Orto** (Corso A Diaz), together with works by greats such as Gano di Fazio and Ambrogio Lorenzetti.

Fonti dell'abbondanza Continue along Via Ximenes until you reach the **Palazzo dell'Abbondanza**, a former public grain storehouse built in 1265 which only recently exposed its most precious secret. In 1999 renovators uncovered the anonymous *Albero della Fecondità* (Tree of Fertility) fresco, depicting a large tree carrying penises as fruits. Women are seen attempting to pick the goods under the threatening watch of a flock of crows. Historians debate the meaning of the artwork – some view it as a hopeful omen to encourage rich harvests, others as a political message warning about the depraved customs of the Ghibellines who opposed the Guelphs and the Pope.

◎ The Garden of Sounds

Not far from Massa Marittima, in the village of Boccheggiano, German contemporary artist Paul Fuchs has set up a permanent exhibition of sculptures known as **Il giardino dei suoni** (The garden of sounds). Scattered on 2 hectares of grassland, the installations made of wood, iron and stone produce unique sounds when they interact with the blowing wind, creating a visual and auditory dialogue between human-built structures and the natural elements of this remote corner of the Tuscan countryside. The garden is on private property; to visit you will need to book by calling 0566998221.

25 The Two Faces of CAPALBIO

SCULPTURE | ARCHITECTURE | CONTEMPORARY ART

In Tuscany's southernmost tip, ancient and contemporary architecture are juxtaposed to form an unusual yet intriguing mix of artistic influences. From the medieval walls of the sleepy hilltop hamlet of Capalbio to the psychedelic colours of the Giardino dei Tarocchi, you'll wonder how such distant worlds managed to collide.

🗺 How to

Getting here Capalbio is easily reached via the E80 motorway and then the Strada Provinciale di Capalbio. From there the Tarot Garden is just 10 minutes southeast.

Public transport The not-too-reliable Tiemme bus 120 runs from Orbetello's train station to Capalbio and the Tarot Garden throughout the day.

Opening hours The Tarot Garden is open 2.30pm to 7.30pm daily from April to mid-October. Buy tickets online at ilgiardinodeitarocchi.it.

Roccapesta (30km);
Terenzi (35km)

SOUTHERN
TUSCANY

Rocca
Aldobrandesca Capalbio

Giardino dei
Tarocchi

Borgo
Carige

Capalbio
Scalo

Lago di Burano
WWF Reserve

L A Z I O

Mediterranean
Sea

N   0   2 km
     0   1 miles

Medieval Capalbio One of Tuscany's most charming *borghi* (hamlets) sits within a dramatic fortification built by the powerful Aldobrandeschi family between the 11th and 12th centuries. Walking on the walls of **Capalbio Alta** offers outstanding views of the coast and the Mediterranean flora of the nearby **Lago di**

Burano WWF Reserve, but it's by getting lost in the labyrinthine stone alleys circling the imposing **Rocca Aldobrandesca** castle that you'll get a sense of life in the town. After that, a glass or two of local Morellino di Scansano wine in one of the local trattorias might offer a new perspective on medieval matters.

The Tarot Garden After visiting Antoni Gaudí's Parc Güell in Barcelona in the 1950s, French-American artist Niki de Saint Phalle (1930–2002) began dreaming of building a park filled with monumental structures inspired by the symbols and figures found on tarot cards. Her vision became reality in 1974, when art collector Marella

ESSEVU/SHUTTERSTOCK ©

Agnelli decided to host Niki de Saint Phalle's project on her family's property in Southern Tuscany. From that moment onward, the **Giardino dei Tarocchi** (Tarot Garden) would absorb all of the artist's energy. Niki de Saint Phalle devoted the rest of her life to building 24 huge colourful figures – includ-

ing a magician, a bishop, a priestess – together with her husband Jean Tinguely. A massive sphinx with the interiors almost entirely covered in mirrors sits in the middle of the park – the artist used this structure as her home while she was working on the garden.

Morellino di Scansano

As you travel toward Capalbio, you'll notice seemingly endless vineyards covering the rolling hills stretching towards the horizon. You are crossing the protected Morellino di Scansano region where the ruby red wine that Maremma is most proud of is made from mostly Sangiovese grapes. Stop by in one of the many *cantine* (wineries) along the way – such as **Roccapesta** (roccapesta.com) or **Terenzi** (terenzi.eu) – for a tasting of Chianti's lesser-known cousin.

Above Capalbio

26 Secluded Coves & **BEACHES**

BEACHES | OUTDOORS | SWIMMING

Tuscany's southern coast offers some of the best beach getaways in the region, with picturesque coves, sandy bays and azure waters surrounded by wild Mediterranean scrublands that offer the ideal balance between relaxation and adventure. Drive down the coast for an off-season seaside escapade.

Above Cala del Gesso (p151)
Right Cala Violina

🗺️ How to

When to go July and August are peak holiday season in Italy and beaches can get packed, especially on weekends. Opt for late spring or early autumn if you'd rather chill in solitude.

Leave no trace Unlike further up the coast, Southern Tuscany features many *spiagge libere* (public beaches), meaning you won't always find facilities such as deckchair rentals, restaurants and toilets. Bring your own supplies and make sure to leave no trace behind.

Map:

Bandite di Scarlino · Braccagni
Cala Violina
Punta Ala · Arcille
Castiglione della Pescaia · **Grosseto**
Spiaggia delle Rocchette · Marina di Grosseto · S O U T H E R N T U S C A N Y
Parco Regionale della Maremma · Alberese
Marina di Alberese · Montiano
Cala di Forno
Mediterranean Sea · Talamone
Albinia
Porto Santo Stefano · Orbetello Scalo
Tyrrhenian Sea · *Cala del Gesso* · **Orbetello**
Monte Argentario · Porto Ercole
Giglio

0 — 10 km
0 — 5 miles

Maremma's Best-Known Cove

The best known of the many *calas* (coves) that dot Maremma's coast is the **Cala Violina**, which takes its name from the violin-like sound produced by the fine sand as you step on it. Part of the **Bandite di Scarlino nature reserve**, the turquoise waters of Cala Violina can be reached via a 4km panoramic walk starting from Portiglioni, by the port of Scarlino, through the pine forest which opens on breathtaking views of the coast. Alternatively, a shorter 2km path starts from the parking lot near the Agriturismo Val Martina (parking €10 per day). Only 700 people are allowed to access the small beach each day; between June and September you will need to reserve your spot by booking via calaviolinascarlino.it.

Relaxation & Water Sports

Eight kilometres north of charming Castiglione della Pescaia and the marshes of the Diaccia Botrona nature reserve, you'll find the long, family-friendly **Spiaggia delle Rocchette**. Stretching all the way to the 12th-century Forte delle Rocchette watchtower, this beach offers the best of both worlds: on one side there's a wide, open sandy area ideal for an undisturbed sun-soaked reading session; on the other, you'll find rocky cliffs perfect for diving and snorkelling in clear waters.

Cala di Forno

Located in the lush Parco Regionale della Maremma, this little golden cove south of Marina di Alberese is embedded in the park's wilderness – a peaceful oasis for those looking to enjoy nature in its raw state, where you might find yourself sharing the fine sands with deer and the sunshine with peregrine falcons. An intense 9km hike through the protected woods of the reserve is necessary to reach

🪦 Caravaggio's Tomb

Legendary artist Michelangelo Merisi, better known as Caravaggio, died in Porto Ercole, Monte Argentario, at age 39 after a short but tumultuous life. After years running away from justice, Caravaggio arrived in Tuscany in 1610 to retrieve a series of paintings mistakenly shipped to Porto Ercole, originally meant to be gifted to the Church in hope of forgiveness for the murder of Ranuccio Tommasoni in 1606. Sick and exhausted, Caravaggio died before being granted a pardon. DNA tests done in 2010 found an 85% chance of Caravaggio's remains being authentic, but the topic remains hotly debated among historians. In 2014 a funerary monument containing the artist's bones was erected in the centre of town. In 2019 it was moved to the local cemetery.

🎬 Maremma in the Movies

The coast of Maremma has formed the backdrop of numerous Hollywood films, including the 22nd episode of the James Bond series *Quantum of Solace* (2008), shot at Villa la Torre in Talamone, and *The Talented Mr Ripley* (1999), which starred Matt Damon and was filmed partly in Porto Ercole.

the tucked-away beach – an experience far different from that of the exclusive seaside resorts of northern Tuscany – but definitely worth the effort.

Tickets to the park need to be purchased in advance at the Alberese Visitor Centre (p135) and a guide is required when visiting between June and September.

Cala del Gesso

The Monte Argentario peninsula has more than 20 beaches and coves to choose from – and its unique geography makes it difficult to decide which one can be said to be the best. Cala del Gesso, found at the end of a steep 700m-long walking path on the western coast, is undoubtedly a good candidate – as you'll notice by driving the 6km panoramic road from Porto Santo Stefano leading to the entrance at the end of Via dei Pionieri. Look up to admire the remains of a 15th-century watchtower still standing on the edge of the cliff, then dive into the azure waters for a close encounter with the rich marine life of the rocky seabed. Don't forget your snorkel!

Left Porto Ercole **Top** Cala di Forno **Above** Spiaggia delle Rocchette

Listings

BEST OF THE REST

🏚 Medieval Hamlets & Spiritual Communities

Seggiano

Famous for the production of one of Tuscany's finest olive oils, Seggiano sits snuggly by Monte Amiata surrounded by secular olive groves. Here you'll also find the open-air museum created by Swiss artist Daniel Spoerri, featuring over 100 installations in a 16-hectare garden.

Santa Fiora

Perched on the southern slope of Monte Amiata, ancient Santa Fiora features fortifications erected by the Aldobrandeschi family who ruled over much of Southern Tuscany during the 11th century.

Rocchette di Fazio

As charming as it is tiny, Rocchette di Fazio hangs on a cliff overlooking the Maremmese countryside. Only a few dozen people inhabit this ancient *borgo* believed to have been occupied by the Knights Templar in the 13th century.

Montemerano

Locked within three layers of ancient city walls, sleepy Montemerano has maintained its medieval character intact over the centuries, with monasteries, churches and urban architecture dating back to the 14th century.

Merigar

International Dzogchen Community stupas, gompas and meditation halls dot the village of Merigar which was founded by Tibetan scholar Chögyal Namkhai Norbu in the nature reserve near the town of Arcidosso. Free tours run regularly for visitors; book via merigar.it.

🏛 Museums of Unexpected Histories

Museo Archeologico e d'Arte della Maremma

Grosseto's MAAM pays tribute to the rich history of the Etruscan civilisation that occupied the region for millennia through authentic artefacts dating back to the 6th century BCE.

Museo Miniere di Mercurio

Mercury mines have played a key role in the economy of Monte Amiata's surroundings since ancient times. This museum in Santa Fiora tells the story of the metal's dangerous extraction process.

MACO Museum

Arcidosso's Museum of Oriental Art & Culture is an exhibition space dedicated to Tibetan art exhibits, gathered by Master Norbu during his career as a professor of Tibetan language and literature at the University of Naples.

🍴 Trattorias, Osterie & Fine Dining

Trattoria Il Giogo   €

A homey eatery in Grosseto known for the generous portions of its seasonal dishes and the delicious desserts. Try the traditional soup *acquacotta,* and complete your meal with a tiramisu.

Tana dei Brilli   €

One of the smallest trattorias you'll come across, Massa Marittima's Tana dei Brilli – literally meaning 'drunks' den' – will conquer your heart and taste buds with its boar-based dishes.

Il Carrettino   €

Chef Andrea Greco brings Sicilian flavours to Tuscany, offering a wide range of vegan and gluten-free options not far from Grosseto's city centre.

Taverna del Vecchio Borgo €€

Brick archways and candlelight form the cosy atmosphere of this rustic restaurant steps away from Massa Marittima's cathedral, knowingly cooking Maremma's specialities.

Grantosco €€

Sophisticated bistro in central Grosseto to enjoy creatively crafted dishes made with locally sourced ingredients, always served with a smile.

Osteria il Recinto €€

Friendly service, relaxed atmosphere, lovely lush garden and tasty, refined cuisine will help you recover from a long day under the sun in Castiglione della Pescaia.

Osteria Canapino €€

With a wine list including over 400 labels, this dimly lit restaurant-slash-enoteca in Grosseto will stimulate your taste buds with new and unexpected flavours matched with the perfect seafood or meat course.

Il Moletto €€

Exceptional ocean views from this Monte Argentario historic restaurant. Operating from Porto Santo Stefano since the 1950s, it pre-pares seafood-based dishes following recipes passed down through generations.

Gabbiano 3.0 €€€

Michelin-starred Gabbiano 3.0 faces the ocean on Marina di Grosseto's port, offering unparalleled gastronomic experiences with a fish-based menu served in a refined space with a Balinese touch.

✿ Winery Explorations & Craft Beer

Rocca di Frassinello

Architect Renzo Piano designed the amphitheatre-shaped cellar where Rocca di Frassinello's barrels are kept for years to allow wines such as Baffonero, Ornello and Poggio alla Guardia to age to perfection.

Val delle Rose

Dedicated to the production of Sangiovese, this winery located in Poggio la Mozza, 15 minutes from Grosseto, opens daily to visitors for tastings of their different interpretations of the local terroir.

Tenuta Ammiraglia

Avant-garde architecture and traditional winemaking come together in this Frescobaldi estate producing both Morellino di Scansano and signature blends from its modern, ship-shaped winery.

Fattoria di Magliano

Award-winning Morellino di Scansano winery in the heart of the wine region, accessible via a cypress-tree-lined countryside road. Don't miss the Heba.

Barbaluppolo

Grosseto's craft beer destination, ideal for a break between Morellino wineries. Ample selection and friendly local crowd on the northern edge of the historical center.

Birrificio La Grada

Visit one of the very few Maremmese brewer-ies near Saturnia, where four different kinds of beer are made with locally grown barley. In-house tastings available on summer evenings.

 Scan to find more things to do in Southern Tuscany online

THE CENTRAL COAST

OUTDOORS | BEACHES | CULTURE

Experience the Central Coast online

● Livorno

Enjoy breathtaking landscape and water views at the **Terrazza Mascagni** in Livorno (p160)

🚆 15mins from Pisa

○ Antignano

Quercianella ○

Ligurian Sea

Fortullino ○

Gorgona

Stroll through the historic city centre of **Rosignano Marittimo** (p167)

🚗 35mins from Livorno

Mediterranean Sea

Take in the sight of Bolgheri's famous **Viale dei Cipressi** (p164)

🚗 1hr from Livorno

THE CENTRAL COAST
Trip Builder

Tyrrhenian Sea

▬▬▬ Whether you want to relax on the sand, delve into centuries-old history or indulge in fresh seafood, Tuscany's central coast has got you covered. With its Etruscan roots, fragrant pine forests and Blue Flag beaches, it's a place where all holiday wishes can come true.

Learn everything about the Etruscans in **Baratti** and **Populonia** (p177)

🚗 15mins from Piombino

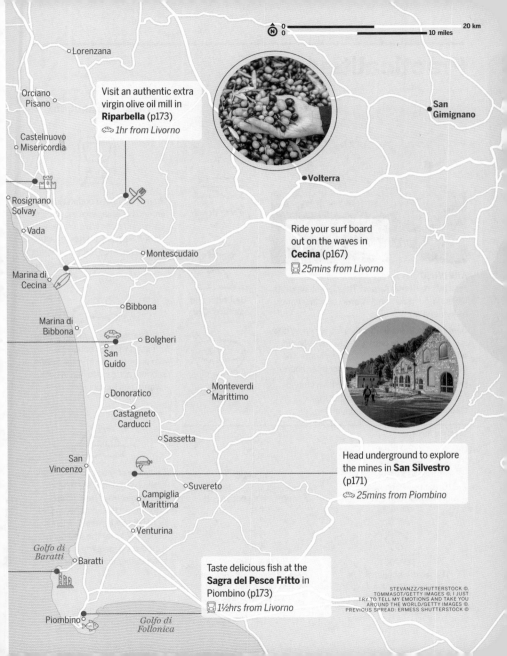

Lorenzana

Orciano
Pisano

Castelnuovo
Misericordia

Rosignano
Solvay

Vada

Marina di
Cecina

Marina di
Bibbona

San
Guido

San
Vincenzo

San
Gimignano

Volterra

Montescudaio

Bibbona

Bolgheri

Donoratico

Castagneto
Carducci

Sassetta

Campiglia
Marittima

Venturina

Baratti

Monteverdi
Marittimo

Suvereto

Golfo di
Baratti

Piombino

Golfo di
Follonica

Visit an authentic extra
virgin olive oil mill in
Riparbella (p173)
🚗 *1hr from Livorno*

Ride your surf board
out on the waves in
Cecina (p167)
🚆 *25mins from Livorno*

Head underground to explore
the mines in **San Silvestro**
(p171)
🚗 *25mins from Piombino*

Taste delicious fish at the
Sagra del Pesce Fritto in
Piombino (p173)
🚆 *1½hrs from Livorno*

0   20 km
0   10 miles

Practicalities

EQROY/SHUTTERSTOCK ©

ARRIVING

Pisa International Airport The closest airport is in Pisa, around 30 minutes away by either car or train from Livorno.

Santa Maria Novella Tuscany's major railway hub is in Florence. Trains depart for Livorno every hour, with the whole trip lasting around 1½ hours. The ride to Piombino takes a little under three hours.

Livorno Centrale Livorno's main train station (pictured) is connected to all other major stations in Tuscany and the rest of Italy.

HOW MUCH FOR A

Ferry ticket
€15

Umbrella and
sunbed €20

Cacciucco
€15

GETTING AROUND

Train A very good option to move around the area since most major towns and cities have a railway station. Intercity trains are faster and pricier, while Regionale trains are convenient but often delayed.

Car Renting your own car, scooter or bike is the best option for exploring the countryside. Rental services are easy to find in both Livorno and Piombino.

Ferry The only way to reach the islands of the Tuscan Archipelago; ferries leave from both Livorno and Piombino, as well as from Elba for the minor islands. Check ahead for the schedule; it changes depending on season and weather conditions.

WHEN TO GO

APR–JUN
Great travelling weather; more crowds pop up as it gets warmer.

JUL–AUG
Peak high season; the sun is never-ending but so is the heat.

SEP–OCT
The weather could still be good, with some luck. Prepare for rain anyway.

NOV–MAR
Low season; proximity to the sea helps keep temperatures somewhat mild.

THE CENTRAL COAST FIND YOUR FEET

EATING & DRINKING

Fish and seafood are, unsurprisingly, a staple of the cuisine of this area of Tuscany. Livorno is famous for its salted cod, known as *baccalà alla livornese* (pictured top), but especially for its *cacciucco* (mixed seafood stew). Tuscany also has its own kind of bread, the *pane sciocco* (pictured bottom), which is famously made without any salt. It takes some getting used to, but it's worth trying with your meals.

Must-try speciality
Purple artichoke, Sagra del Carciofo (p173), Riotorto

Best olive oil degustation
La Melatina (p174)

THE CENTRAL COAST FIND YOUR FEET

CONNECT & FIND YOUR WAY

Wi-fi It's easier to find free wi-fi in major towns compared to the countryside where it's sometimes even difficult to get data.

Navigation Head to tourist offices for a paper map, or look for public maps displayed around city and village centres. Digital maps might not be accurate when it comes to little medieval streets or countryside roads.

WHERE TO STAY

From all-inclusive beach resorts to tranquil *agriturismi* (farm-stay accommodation), you have several options when deciding where to stop and rest during your trip along the coast. Many towns can also be visited on a day trip from Pisa.

Place	Pro/Con
Livorno	The major city in the area with plenty of things to do and see; can be crowded and noisy.
Rosignano	Your best bet at an Italian summer experience of hotels and beaches; no shortage of crowds during high season.
Castagneto Carducci	Stay in an *agriturismo* in the surrounding hills for utter peace; a car or scooter is a must-have.
Elba (Tuscan Archipelago)	The most scenic location you can choose; careful planning is needed.

BEACH RESORTS

Most beach resorts along the coast open around 8am and close around 8pm, unless they also have a nightclub that stays open well into the morning.

MONEY

You'll have no issues finding ATMs in major towns but the same does not apply to smaller villages. Some places, especially in the countryside, will only accept cash.

27 Seafaring
LIVORNO

HISTORY | CULTURE | CITY WALK

Born out of the Medici's sheer force of will during the Renaissance, Livorno quickly grew to become one of the most international and culturally diverse cities in the country, welcoming immigrants and refugees from every corner of the Mediterranean. Come and see the legacy that both the waves and the Medici family have left behind.

📍 How to

Getting here Livorno is easy to reach by regional train as a day trip out of Florence (one hour and 40 minutes) and Pisa (15 minutes).

When to go Visit in early spring or early autumn to maximise your chances of good weather without extreme heat or crowds.

Must-try dish Seafood rules supreme over Livorno cuisine; you can't leave the city without trying its famous *cacciucco*, a tomato-based seafood soup served with bread.

The sea is history Livorno's placement along the Tuscan coast has always had major strategic importance – which is why the Medici orchestrated for it to become their domain's main port. Enjoy a breathtaking view of that all-important sea at the waterfront **Terrazza Mascagni**, with its characteristic checkered tiles, then

head into the historic heart of the city, the neighbourhood of **Venezia Nuova**. Here you can get lost walking alongside its canals and feel centuries come alive at the 16th-century **Fortezza Vecchia** and **Fortezza Nuova**, the two forts that have played a major role in defending the city throughout the centuries.

Understanding the city Dive into the **Mercato delle Vettovaglie**, one of the biggest in Europe, built to echo Parisian architecture, then head to the restaurant located at its centre **Alle Vettovaglie** to enjoy a modern twist on the city's traditional cuisine such as *panini* filled with seafood. Afterwards, you might want to check out

VITI/GETTY IMAGES ©

the **Mediterranean Natural History Museum** and its marine and wildlife exhibits, especially if you're travelling with little ones.

Beach break If you want to dip your toes in, there are several beaches around Livorno that have obtained the prestigious Blue Flag award, certifying their cleanliness and sustainability. Lie down at **Calafuria** or **Quercianella**, both less than half an hour by train south from Livorno, where you can also go snorkelling or surfing, and take a mind-clearing walk in the Mediterranean bush further inland.

⚓ Sea Races

Livorno has no shortage of water-bound rowing races taking place between its various neighbourhood teams. The season starts with the centuries-old **Palio dell'Antenna** (21 May) in the city's harbour followed by the **Coppa Risiatori** (second Sunday of June), further out at sea, and the **Coppa Barontini** (last Saturday of June), which takes place at night on the city's canals. Finally it's time for the **Palio Marinaro** (second Sunday of July), which was officially created at the start of the 20th century but is inspired by much older races; secure a spot on the Terrazza Mascagni to watch the teams sail by.

Above Fortezza Vecchia

LIGHTING
the Way

POSTCARD

PLACE STAMP

01 The Lamp
The Livorno Lighthouse, the oldest in the country, has been in use since the Middle Ages.

02 Lights off
The Rio Marina lighthouse, on the isle of Elba, lived and died during the 20th century; it's recognisable by its battlements.

03 Lancet arch
The still-active Piombino lighthouse, built on the spot of an old defensive fortification, boasts a unique neo-Gothic architectural style.

04 Sea semaphore
The old semaphore on the isle of Capraia, active from the 1910s until the 1950s, also served as a meteorological station.

05 Red and white
The lighthouse on the isle of Giannutri, sitting right on the Grottoni cliffs, is very similar to the one on the isle of Giglio.

06 Nice neighbourhood
The Porteferraio lighthouse, on the isle of Elba, also sits within the complex of a Renaissance fort, the Forte Stella.

07 Sea buddies
Off the shores of Livorno, two lighthouses mark the Meloria shallows. This stretch of sea also houses a single watchtower, built and rebuilt since the 12th century.

08 Unmissable
Sailors can see the southern tip of the isle of Giglio thanks to the Capel Rosso lighthouse, painted in bright white and red.

09 Vantage point
The isle of Pianosa is very flat – the lamp of its lighthouse is the highest point on the entire island.

10 Above a fort
The lighthouse at Porto Ercole, on the Argentario Peninsula, is built on top of the 12th-century Rocca Aldobrandesca.

28 ARTFUL
Cypresses

CULTURE | OUTDOORS | LITERATURE

The villages and towns that dot the Costa degli Etruschi, stretching from Livorno to Piombino, have inspired artists and poets for centuries, and feature in some of the most famous pieces of Italian art and literature. With their peaceful landscapes, triumphant nature and twisting, cobbled streets filled with myriad scents and sounds, it's easy to see why.

🗺 How to

Getting around You can reach the main villages (such as Castagneto Carducci and Rosignano Marittimo) via train, but the countryside is best explored on four or two wheels.

When to go Summer is glorious but can be extremely hot. Late spring and early autumn are also lovely.

Feeling expensive If you want to really splurge on something, consider a bottle of Sassicaia, one of the world's most exclusive reds and a Super Tuscan wine produced right in this area.

Carducci's words The picturesque village of **Castagneto Carducci** is named after Giosuè Carducci (1835–1907), one of Italy's most famous poets, and here you can visit the house he lived in, the aptly named **Museo Casa Carducci** (carduccicastagneto. wordpress.com). Once you're done strolling around the village, whose atmosphere returns time and time again in Carducci's poems, head out to one of the most famous places that have inspired his works: the famous **Viale dei Cipressi** on the road to **Bolgheri**, with its perfect – and very photogenic – cypresses lining the streets.

The Macchiaioli's paintings The village of **Castiglioncello**, a fraction of the town of Rosignano Marittimo, was the unofficial headquarters of the Macchiaioli, a group of Italian painters that refused to follow the conventions of 19th-century art. The **Castello Pasquini** now stands where their unofficial

THE CENTRAL COAST EXPERIENCES

🚴 Off to the Races!

The Tuscan countryside might inspire tranquil relaxation and peaceful contemplation, but it also offers the chance to get your blood pumping. If you're the proud owner of a bike made before 1987 then you're eligible to participate in the **Etrusca Ciclostorica** (etruscaciclostorica.it) in April, a bike race around the area of Castagneto Carducci open to both professionals and amateurs with plenty of routes to choose from. If you're more of a runner than a biker then there's also the **Bolgheri Run** (bolgherirun.com) in May, a half marathon – but there's also a shortened 9km route – open to registered athletes.

headquarters used to be and serves as a venue for events and concerts; check the calendar at local tourist offices to see if there's anything interesting happening when you're there.

The entire area surrounding Castiglioncello inspired the works of the Macchiaioli, including the villages of Castelnuovo, Gabbro and Nibbiaia, also Rosignano Marittimo fractions, as well as the natural sights of the Monte Pelato, the Pineta Marradi and the Baia del Quercetano, all worth a trek to mix culture with a fun day outdoors.

Above Viale dei Cipressi

29 Beach LIFE

BEACHES | OUTDOORS | SWIMMING

Named after the fascinating and still-mysterious Etruscan people who once inhabited this area of Tuscany, the Costa degli Etruschi is peak Mediterranean excellence. Everywhere you turn there's picture-perfect scenery, thrilling water activities, delicious food and good old-fashioned sunbathing.

Above Bibbona (p168) **Right** Flamingo, Riserva Naturale Orti di Bottagone (p169)

How to

Getting around
You can easily move around via regional trains, which stop at every town and city along the coast. See costaetruska.it.

When to go Peak summer season starts from the middle of June and ends with August. September still has some decent weather and fewer crowds.

Top tip The Costa degli Etruschi is perfect for van lifers – camping spots like **Pappasole** (pappasole.it) are very easy to find.

Rosignano Marittimo
Rosignano Solvay
Parco dei Poggetti
Riparbella
Ligurian Sea
Vada
Montescudaio
Pescecotto
Marina di Cecina
Cecina *Fore 74*
Macchia della Magona
Bibbona
Marina di Bibbona
Villa Romana San Vincenzino
Costa degli Etruschi
Castagneto Carducci
Serendipity
San Vincenzo
Tyrrhenian Sea
Campiglia Marittima
Venturina
Populonia
Baratti
Riserva Naturale Orti di Bottagone
Piombino
Golfo di Follonica
0 — 10 km
0 — 5 miles

Beach & More

One of the first towns on the Costa degli Etruschi and an hour-ish by train away from Livorno, **Rosignano Solvay** and **Rosignano Marittimo** offer you the best of both worlds – paradise beaches to sprawl on and heaps of culture to discover. Stroll around the medieval city centre and marvel at the landscape you can enjoy from the vantage point of the **Parco dei Poggetti**. If you happen to visit in August, peek at the **Tre civette sul comò festival** (prolocorosignanomarittimo.it), with acrobats and performers taking over the town's streets.

Surfing Hour

The town of **Cecina** has been populated for centuries, well before the start of the Roman Empire. The sandy, wide beaches of its marina are perfect for relaxing or trying your best on a board. Plenty of schools – such as **Spot1** (spot1.it) and **Corsi KiteSurf** (corsikitesurf.com) – offer surfing and kitesurfing lessons for beginners, or you can head out by yourself if you feel confident enough. And if you get tired of the sun and the sea, head into the city centre to pay a visit to the Roman villa **San Vincenzino** for some classical history.

Beaches & Pine Forests

The marina in **Bibbona** is one of the most beloved of the entire Costa degli Etruschi. You'll find something to match your taste here, whether you like free, wild beaches or fully organised, comfortable resorts. The coast around Bibbona is also bordered by a massive pine forest, perfect for a relaxing walk after a long day spent at the beach. If you want to add some more adrenaline, opt for one of the many hikes crossing the natural reserve of the **Macchia della Magona**, which you can follow on foot, by bike or even on horseback.

🐟 Hunting Seafood

What's better than sitting down for a fish dinner with a glass of fresh white wine after a day at the beach? All towns along the Costa degli Etruschi have great restaurants for you to indulge in local delicacies. You'll never be at risk of not finding the perfect spot.

Serendipity (serendipity sanvincenzo.it) Excellent fresh seafood with a spectacular view of the waves at sunset in San Vincenzo.

Pescecotto (pescecotto. com) Traditional dishes and evergreen pizza right in the Cecina harbour.

Forte 74 (facebook.com/ forte74marinadibibbona) Fresh seafood steps away from the sea in Bibbona.

Il Cardellino (ilcardellino. net) The perfect all-day location in Castiglioncello.

STEVANZZ/SHUTTERSTOCK ©

ALESSANDRA ATES/EYEEM/GETTY IMAGES ©

🐾 Pet-Friendly

Travelling with your four-legged best friend? For some fun in the sun together, head to **San Vincenzo's Dog Beach** (dog-beach.it) and to **Perelli's Bagno Pascià** (bagnopascia.it) for all-inclusive resorts, or to the free beaches in Rosignano Solvay and Marina di Bibbona.

Walls & Sights

The history of **Piombino** goes back centuries to the Etruscan times, from the city walls that might have been designed by Leonardo da Vinci himself to the centre's winding medieval streets leading down to the **Porto Vecchio**, the old harbour, protected by a natural rock formation. Stop at **Piazza Bovio** on a clear, sunny day to spot the islands of the Tuscan Archipelago, as well as Corsica beyond them, and then go lie down on one of the many beaches the area has to offer – take your pick among small *calette* (coves) and wide stretches of sand.

For a break from the waves, hike up to the **Populonia** acropolis, part of what was the only Etruscan city to look out directly onto the sea, or explore one of the natural reserves such as **Parco Naturale di Montioni** or the **Riserva Naturale Orti di Bottagone** for your chance at seeing its pink flamingos.

I JUST TRY TO TELL MY EMOTIONS AND TAKE YOU AROUND THE WORLD/GETTY IMAGES ©

Left Beach, San Vincenzo **Top** View from Piazza Bovio, Piombino **Above** Windsurfer, Marina di Cecina (p167)

30 Wandering the PARKS

OUTDOORS | NATURE | ADVENTURE

■■■■ The coastal area of Tuscany and the province of Livorno boast several natural parks and protected reserves, perfect for relaxing in nature, doing some animal-watching or exploring an abandoned mine.

ATLANTIDE PHOTOTRAVEL/GETTY IMAGES ©

🗺 Trip Notes

Getting around The best option is to rent your own four wheels. You can find car-hire services in Livorno and Piombino.

When to go Mid- to late spring is the best. If you visit in summer be sure to have everything you need to combat heat and sunburn.

Top tip The Val di Cornia parks offer you discounts and advantages with the pArcheo Card.

🌿 Purple Fields

If visiting in June and July, take a detour inland and head to the stretch of road that connects the villages of **Orciano Pisano** and **Santa Luce** – then stop and take in the absolutely breathtaking view of the lavender fields in full bloom.

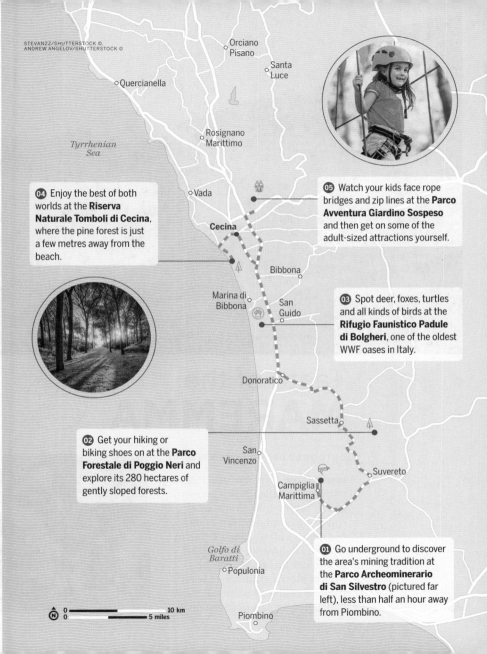

STEVANZZ/SHUTTERSTOCK ©,
ANDREW ANGELOV/SHUTTERSTOCK ©

Quercianella

Orciano
Pisano

Santa
Luce

*Tyrrhenian
Sea*

Rosignano
Marittimo

Vada

Cecina

Bibbona

04 Enjoy the best of both worlds at the **Riserva Naturale Tomboli di Cecina**, where the pine forest is just a few metres away from the beach.

05 Watch your kids face rope bridges and zip lines at the **Parco Avventura Giardino Sospeso** and then get on some of the adult-sized attractions yourself.

Marina di Bibbona

San Guido

03 Spot deer, foxes, turtles and all kinds of birds at the **Rifugio Faunistico Padule di Bolgheri**, one of the oldest WWF oases in Italy.

Donoratico

Sassetta

02 Get your hiking or biking shoes on at the **Parco Forestale di Poggio Neri** and explore its 280 hectares of gently sloped forests.

San Vincenzo

Suvereto

Campiglia Marittima

01 Go underground to discover the area's mining tradition at the **Parco Archeominerario di San Silvestro** (pictured far left), less than half an hour away from Piombino.

Golfo di Baratti

Populonia

0   10 km
0   5 miles

Piombino

31 Taste of the MAREMMA

OUTDOORS | FOOD | COUNTRYSIDE

■■■ Close your eyes and imagine picturesque villages perched on gentle rolling hills, swept by a soft evening breeze after a long hot day. It's all waiting for you in the Livorno inland, aptly called Maremma Livornese. It's the perfect place to indulge in some rural relaxation, traditional meals and a glass or two of red wine.

Above Casale Marittimo (p174)
Right Purple artichoke

🗺️ How to

Getting around Get the most out of your wandering on four and two wheels. You can find rental services in Livorno and Piombino.

When to go Autumn is lovely, with the wine-harvest season in full swing and many events happening from September onward.

Bread stop Cross into the province of Pisa to taste authentic Tuscan bread, *pane sciocco,* in the village of **Montescudaio**, the City of Wine and Bread.

Foodie Festivals

There are few better ways to celebrate food than at a *sagra,* a festival dedicated to one specific dish or ingredient – and there's plenty of them in the Maremma Livornese. Hunt for the best and freshest fish at the **Sagra del Pesce Fritto** in Piombino or at the **Festa del Pescatore** in Cecina – both happening in September. If you're not a fan of seafood, then head to Sassetta for the **Feste d'Ottobre**, which, as the name suggests, takes place around the middle of October, to enjoy traditional dishes made of venison and seasonal produce such as chestnuts and mushrooms.

In November, the villages of Riparbella and Suvereto gear up for their respective **Sagre del Cinghiale** – stop for a delicious dish of boar meat, medieval-inspired street shows and lots of artisanal shopping. Vegetarians, fear not; head to Riotorto and Venturina Terme towards the middle of April for two events, the **Sagra del Carciofo** and the **Carciofo Pride**, dedicated entirely to the very local purple artichoke.

The Wonders of Oil

The Maremma Livornese isn't only about the wine, seafood and venison – the whole area is also known and appreciated for its olive oil production. Finding an oil mill to tour is an easy feat and one that goes hand in hand with a more 'classic' winery visit. Head to the oil mill of **La Melatina** (terretruria.it) in Riparbella to discover how olive oil is made and, of course, taste a delicious degustation.

The areas around **Guardistallo** and **Casale Marittimo** – which also happens to be on the Most Beautiful Italian Towns list – also have their fair share of oil mills to visit, like **Podere Il Montaleo** (podereilmontaleo.it).

A Touch of History

The villages and towns of the Maremma Livornese have been standing for centuries, and each of their streets carries the weight

🍇 Grapes Heaven

Tuscan wines are famous and well loved around the world. You can often find the best regional wines at local restaurants, but if you want a more in-depth wine-seeking adventure follow one of the **Strade del Vino** (stradevinodi toscana.it) itineraries that criss-cross the entire region. The **Strada in the Costa degli Etruschi** (lastradadelvino.com) maps the entire area and is the perfect way to discover which wineries are open for an ultimate visit and degustation combo.

ROBERTONENCINI/SHUTTERSTOCK ©

BARMALINI/SHUTTERSTOCK ©

I JUST TRY TO TELL MY EMOTIONS AND TAKE YOU AROUND THE WORLD/GETTY IMAGES ©

Instagram Worthy

For a truly unique holiday shot, head to the village of **Peccioli**, 45 minutes by car from Livorno, for its pastel-coloured houses and the modern art installations popping up on its hillside.

of history dating back to the Etruscans and the Romans. Between one seafood lunch here and one venison dinner there you'll have plenty to explore. Walk along the walls of **Montescudaio** to enjoy a breathtaking view over the countryside and feel like a medieval guard watching for an enemy attack then stop for lunch at the restaurant **Il Frantoio**. The fort in the centre of **Campiglia Marittima** is an open-air museum and a masterclass in medieval architecture. The village of **Santa Luce** is a labyrinth of little streets that may or may not have been a headquarters for the Knights Templar. The city centre in **Sassetta** is dotted with red marble sculptures waiting to be discovered.

Left Vineyard, Costa degli Etruschi **Top** Montescudaio **Above** Olive oil tasting

32 Tracing Etruscan STEPS

ARCHAEOLOGY | HISTORY | CULTURE

▬▬▬ Before the Romans there were the mysterious and fascinating Etruscans, who prospered in Tuscany between the 10th and 1st century BCE and left their mark all over ancient culture. Here's where to trace the legacy of their incredibly refined culture along the coast that bears their name.

DEAGOSTINI/GETTY IMAGES ©

🗺 Trip Notes

Getting around You can easily reach Piombino by train, but the best way to get to the smaller towns is renting a car.

When to go Visit in late spring or early autumn for your best chance at nice weather without extreme heat.

How much The average entrance fee is €10 for a full-price ticket and €8 for a reduced price one.

♨ Bathe Like an Etruscan

Etruscans knew how to enjoy life's pleasures, and that included a relaxing spa day. If you want to follow their example then head to the **Baths of Venturina** (termediventurina.it), already well-known in Etruscan days for the amazing qualities of their thermal waters – stable at 45°C, they're particularly well suited to help with respiratory and skin issues.

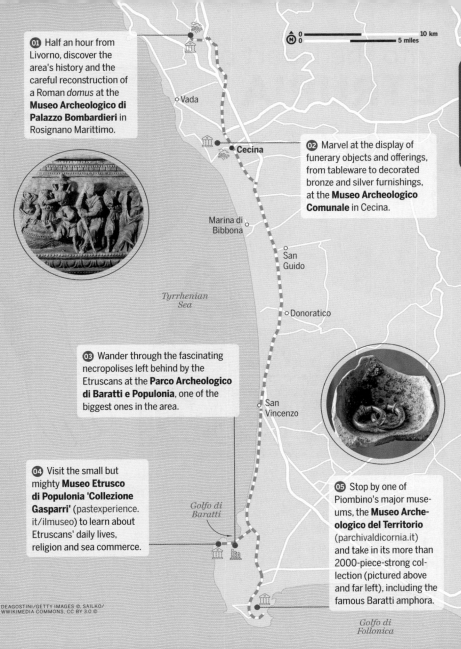

01 Half an hour from Livorno, discover the area's history and the careful reconstruction of a Roman *domus* at the **Museo Archeologico di Palazzo Bombardieri** in Rosignano Marittimo.

02 Marvel at the display of funerary objects and offerings, from tableware to decorated bronze and silver furnishings, at the **Museo Archeologico Comunale** in Cecina.

03 Wander through the fascinating necropolises left behind by the Etruscans at the **Parco Archeologico di Baratti e Populonia**, one of the biggest ones in the area.

04 Visit the small but mighty **Museo Etrusco di Populonia 'Collezione Gasparri'** (pastexperience. it/ilmuseo) to learn about Etruscans' daily lives, religion and sea commerce.

05 Stop by one of Piombino's major museums, the **Museo Archeologico del Territorio** (parchivaldicornia.it) and take in its more than 2000-piece-strong collection (pictured above and far left), including the famous Baratti amphora.

Vada

Cecina

Marina di Bibbona

San Guido

Tyrrhenian Sea

Donoratico

San Vincenzo

Golfo di Baratti

Golfo di Follonica

0 10 km
0 5 miles

Into the Heart of
ETRURIA

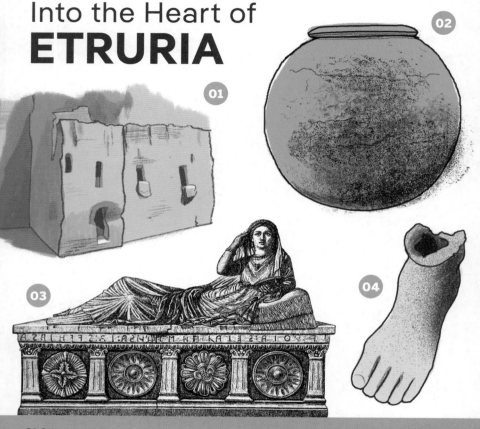

01 Stone tombs
Etruscan tombs were also carved into stone, such as the ones that remain in the Populonia necropolis.

02 Precious goods
A *dolio*, like the one at the Collezione Gasparri museum (p177) in Populonia, was a clay container to store or transport food, oil and wine.

03 A likeness
Etruscan dead were buried in elaborate and engraved sarcophagi, which often represented the face and body of the deceased.

04 Praying for help
Reproductions of various body parts were left for the gods to ask for their help in healing specific ailments and illnesses.

05 Sea people
Etruscans were sea-faring people – anchors made of stone were an essential item on every Etruscan boat.

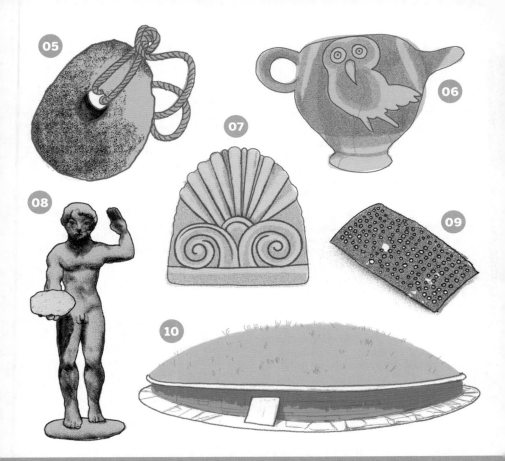

06 Wisdom owl
The Etruscan goddess Menrva later became the Roman Minerva – both were represented by her sacred animal, the owl.

07 Greek friends
This engraving of a little palm, located on a funerary stele, has a lot of Greek artistic influence, showing how strong the relationship between Etruscans and Greeks was.

08 A disc thrower
This bronze statuette found in the Populonia necropolis was believed to be a man carrying a plate – turns out he's actually a discobolus.

09 Spice it up
Etruscans used bronze graters like this to shred the spices they were going to mix with wine during their beloved symposiums.

10 Otherworldly grandeur
Etruscan burial mounds were no small affair, especially if they belonged to aristocrats— like the Tomba dei Carri in the Populonia necropolis (p177).

Listings

BEST OF THE REST

Eating Local

Ristorante Il Bucaniere €€

The Il Bucaniere in San Vincenzo serves a seasonal menu that consists of locally sourced fish, more often than not procured by the restaurant's owner, as well as meat dishes – all to be enjoyed while looking out at sea.

Osteria Enoteca San Guido €€€

The Osteria Enoteca San Guido, located in Bolgheri, is connected to the Tenuta San Guido – the birthplace of one of the most exclusive wines in the world, the Sassicaia. The Osteria's seasonal menu is planned around good wine, and you can be sure to drink plenty of it here.

Locanda dell'Aioncino €€

Lost in the middle of the Bibbona countryside, the Locanda dell'Aioncino's menu features locally produced traditional dishes, which, of course, vary according to what's in season. The location is also a rustic chic dream come true.

Osteria Il Sigillo €€

Rosignano's Osteria Il Sigillo is the place to go for some excellent steak – it even has a decalogue to make sure you enjoy it to the max – as well as a wide selection of both mains and traditional pasta shapes and sauces.

Must-Try Snacks

Antica Friggitoria Il Frataio €

When in Livorno, head to the Antica Friggitoria Il Frataio to try the *frate,* a local snack that resembles a doughnut and is served straight from the fryer after being dipped in sugar. The menu also includes the *scagliozzi,* chunks of polenta left to dry and then fried.

Conca d'Oro Cioccolateria €€

After a long soak in the natural thermal springs of Venturina Terme, head to the Conca d'Oro Cioccolateria for a delicious chocolate-based snack. Pick whatever catches your fancy from the many original creations.

Al Polpo Marino €

Located right on the Baratti beach, the little Al Polpo Marino kiosk serves up piping hot fish-and-octopus fry with a side dish of French fries. It's the perfect stop for either lunch or *aperitivo* after a day of sand and sea.

Wine & Oil Degustations

Ca' Marcanda

Winemaking tradition meets state-of-the-art architectural design at Ca' Marcanda, a winery that is almost completely built underground and makes for a unique tasting experience.

Tenuta Argentiera

Looking out onto the sea, the Tenuta Argentiera is a triumph of nature. You can

Tenuta dell'Ornellaia

visit its estate and cellar and then enjoy a tasting with breathtaking views to the Tyrrhenian Sea.

Tenuta dell'Ornellaia

The estate lies on a particularly rich terrain, meaning it can easily produce both red and white wines of excellent quality. Each year's vintage also features a new label designed by an international artist.

Piccolo Frantoio di Bolgheri

As the name suggests, the Piccolo Frantoio di Bolgheri is small but mighty. A family business, it produces three different varieties of extra virgin olive oil and offers visits to the estate and oil tastings.

Antico Frantoio Toscano

A family business dating back to the 19th century, this oil mill focuses exclusively on the production of extra virgin olive oil. Taste it after a visit of the estate and mill.

L'Antico Frantoio di Segalari

Focused on sustainable oil production and advanced technologies, the Antico Frantoio di Segalari also doubles as an *agriturismo* and a restaurant for a delightful stay surrounded by nature.

Water Sports

Inkite School

Located in Vada, the Inkite School offers individual kitesurfing lessons for all levels, close to the shore and out at sea. Classes run from April until October, weather permitting.

Tutun Club

The Tutun Club in San Vincenzo is the place to go for all kinds of water activities, from windsurfing to snorkelling to paddleboating. It also rents equipment so you can venture out solo.

Tombolo Talasso & Beach Resort

Etruscan Spa Days

Calidario Terme Etrusche Resort & Spa

Reaping all the benefits of the historic Venturina Terme thermal waters, Calidario Terme Etrusche Resort & Spa features an impressive natural pool as well as the indoor Thermarium, with a magnificent arched ceiling.

La Cerreta Terme

Sassetta is another famous thermal location along the Costa degli Etruschi, and at Cerreta, located inside the natural park of Poggio Neri, you'll be able to enjoy both the power of thermal waters as well as locally farmed produce.

Tombolo Talasso & Beach Resort

Located in Marina di Castagneto Carducci, Tombolo Talasso & Beach Resort takes inspiration from its proximity to the sea and offers a wide range of thalassotherapy treatments in a unique location inspired by an underwater grotto.

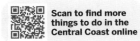
Scan to find more things to do in the Central Coast online

CLAUDIO BEDUSCHI/AGF/UNIVERSAL IMAGES GROUP VIA GETTY IMAGES ©

33 The Many Faces
OF ELBA

ISLANDS | OUTDOORS | HISTORY

■■■■■ The isle of Elba is the main island of the Tuscan Archipelago and the third largest in Italy after Sicily and Sardinia. Both natural paradise and imperial prison, once you step off the ferry from the mainland you will find beautiful beaches, delicious food, stunning landscapes and a fascinating history.

ESSEVU/SHUTTERSTOCK ©

🗺 How to

Getting here Ferries sail throughout the year from Piombino to two of Elba's main settlements, Portoferraio and Rio Marina. It's a good idea to book in advance during the high season.

When to go To avoid the summer heat and crowds, consider a visit in late spring or early autumn.

Getting around The best way to move around on the island is having your own wheels; car and scooter rentals are located in Portoferraio and other major towns.

IMAGEBROKER/FRANK SCHNEIDER/GETTY IMAGES ©

Textbook Mediterranean

The isle of Elba is one of those quintessentially Mediterranean places where your only real issue will be choosing which beach you want to hit up first. If you're looking for absolute isolation and picturesque sights, then head to the **Spiaggia di Fonza** on the southern side of the isle (just outside of Marina di Campo) or to the **Cala della Cotaccia**, on the western tip of Elba. If you're travelling with children or you prefer a more seaside town vibe, then try **Marciana Marina**, on the northern side, and **Porto Azzurro**, on the eastern side.

If you're seeking something more thrilling, head to **Pomonte** to dive the submerged wreck of the *Elviscot,* a small merchant ship which sunk here in the early '70s after all of its crew managed to escape. The dive is relatively easy, since the wreck lies at just 12m under

CHERRYBLOSSOM/SHUTTERSTOCK ©

🍷 Cin Cin!

The only distillery on Elba, the **Smania** (smanialiquori. it), produces a wide array of digestifs made from local produce like lemons and myrtle. If you're looking for the perfect way to accompany your dinner, look no further than the locally produced wine (the DOCG Elba Aleatico Passito) – a staple at every Elba restaurant.

Above left Portoferraio (p185) **Above right** *Elviscot* wreck, Pomonte **Left** Red admiral, Butterfly Sanctuary (p184)

the surface, but the actual exploration of the ship is suggested only to expert divers.

All the Nature, All the Time

Just because you're on an island doesn't mean you have to spend all of your time in the water. The typical Mediterranean bush of the isle of Elba can also be explored by bike or hiking (make sure you bring plenty of water and sunscreen). The **Capoliveri Bike Park** (capoliveribikepark.it) has a variety of routes so you can choose the one that matches your level of expertise. That same area also has a rich tradition of mining and makes for some interesting treks. Choose from one of the many paths that trace the miners' step, such as the one leading to the old **Mines of Calamita**, some three hours out of Capoliveri, and head out by yourself or with a guide (see minieredicalamita.it). The island also has a **Butterfly Sanctuary**, which is home to some species that were once thought to be extinct.

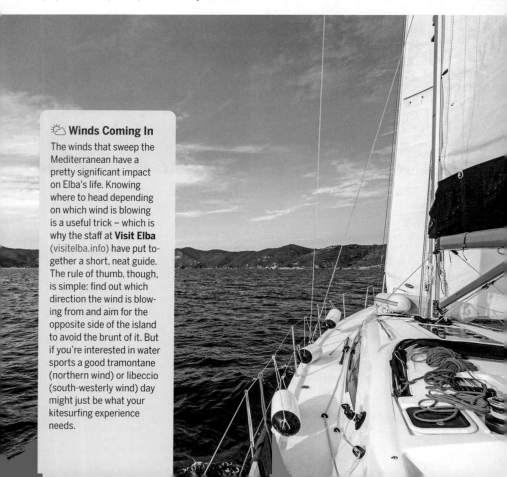

☁ Winds Coming In

The winds that sweep the Mediterranean have a pretty significant impact on Elba's life. Knowing where to head depending on which wind is blowing is a useful trick – which is why the staff at **Visit Elba** (visitelba.info) have put together a short, neat guide. The rule of thumb, though, is simple: find out which direction the wind is blowing from and aim for the opposite side of the island to avoid the brunt of it. But if you're interested in water sports a good tramontane (northern wind) or libeccio (south-westerly wind) day might just be what your kitesurfing experience needs.

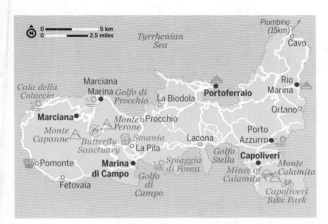

Left Sailing off Elba
Below Palazzina dei Mulini

An Emperor in Exile

You can't get a full picture of the isle of Elba without knowing one of its most famous residents – Napoleon Bonaparte, emperor of the French in the 19th century, who was exiled on the island. He lived here for 10 months, before escaping and returning to France for his final 100 days (after which he was exiled to the much more secluded isle of St Helena, surrounded by nothing but the Atlantic Ocean). If you want to take a break from sunbathing and hiking for some historical touring, you can easily trace Napoleon's footsteps in his two main residences in **Portoferraio**, Elba's main town: the **Palazzina dei Mulini** and the **Villa San Martino**.

34 Sail to Tuscan
ISLANDS

ISLANDS | OUTDOORS | NATURE

The Tuscan Archipelago includes seven main islands, from Elba, the country's third-largest island, to small jewels like Giannutri and Montecristo, through to the equally gorgeous isles of Giglio, Capraia, Pianosa and Gorgona. Surrounded by a cloud of islets and reefs, the archipelago is the place to totally disconnect.

K - PHOTO/SHUTTERSTOCK ©

🗺 How to

Getting here Several ferry companies sail to the islands of the archipelago from the mainland, in particular Piombino, Livorno and Porto Santo Stefano. Some islands are also reachable from Rio Marina on Elba. Your departure point will be different depending on which island you want to reach.

When to go Crossings are more regular in the warmer months than they are in autumn and winter.

Where to stay Elba and Giglio are very good options to base yourself in; check in advance at islepark.it.

DEAGOSTINI/GETTY IMAGES ©

Lily of the Sea

The isle of **Giglio** is the second largest in the archipelago after the isle of Elba (p182), but it's still small – its entire surface is just a bit more than 20 sq km. But that doesn't mean you'll find yourself with nothing to do – if you manage to get a hold of some wheels, then you can start exploring. The isle has three main villages, and all offer some unique sights. **Giglio Porto**, where ferries arrive, is the oldest village on the isle with plenty of Roman ruins to visit. Then there's **Giglio Castello**, where time seems to have stopped in the 12th century; take a walk along the city walls, which saw many battles between the islanders and pirates that were coming from the sea. Finally, head over to **Giglio Campese**, the tourist hub of the isle, to enjoy some nightlife.

GIOAPPIANI/SHUTTERSTOCK ©

 Volcanic Remains

Capraia was created by a volcanic eruption and you can still see the gap that it left on its southern side. After being left open to the elements for millennia, the cliffside has turned into a distinctive red colour, which is why the whole area is called **Cala Rossa**.

Above left Boats off Giglio coastline **Above right** Villa Domizia, Giannutri (p188) **Left** Caldane beach (p188), Giglio

If you want to lie under the sun, head to **Cannelle**, **Caldane** or **Arenella**. All three of these sandy beaches are within walking distance from Giglio Porto and feature beach resorts to relax in as well as an interesting underwater life to explore for both kids and adults.

From the Romans to Us

Both Pianosa and Giannutri, the smallest of the seven islands of the Tuscan Archipelago, have some interesting Roman history to tell.

On **Pianosa** visit what is left of Christian catacombs dating back to the 4th century CE, as well as a 1st century CE Roman residence that saw some blood during the reign of Emperor Augustus. Afterwards, take a dip in **Cala Giovanna**, the only beach on the isle where you're allowed to swim. **Giannutri** – sacred to Diana, goddess of the hunt and the moon, because of its distinct half-moon shape – hosts the remains of a beautiful Roman villa, **Villa Domizia**, located at one of the isle's two main

⛴ Special Entry

Visiting **Montecristo** and **Gorgona** might not be as easy as the rest of the archipelago. The former is a natural reserve with highly regulated access, and less than 2000 people are allowed to visit each year. The latter is an active penitentiary colony, and a maximum of 100 people are allowed per day. The wait lists are somewhat long and there are strict conditions that need to be met before you can book your place, but both islands are worth the wait, especially if you love hiking. All information is available at parcoarcipelago.info.

Gorgona

Cecina

Mediterranean Sea

Pelagos Sanctuary for Cetaceans

Capraia

Tuscan Archipelago

●**Massa Marittima**

Elba

●**Grosseto**

Pianosa

Tyrrhenian Sea

CORSICA

Montecristo

Giglio

●**Orbetello**

Giannutri

0   20 km
0   10 miles

STEFANO73/SHUTTERSTOCK ©

Left Montecristo **Below**
Cratena peregrina off Pianosa

KABBAPHOTOS/GETTY IMAGES ©

docking spots, **Cala Maestra**. You can hike the distance that separates it from **Cala Spalmatoio** to enjoy Giannutri's wild nature.

Fauna Extraordinaire

The entire Tuscan Archipelago is part of a natural park, meaning you'll have the chance of catching sight of some truly amazing fauna in its natural habitat. The isle of Pianosa, for example, is the perfect spot for birdwatching (especially birds of prey) and diving to look at sea creatures like fish and crustaceans. Importantly, the entire archipelago also sits within the **Pelagos Sanctuary for Cetaceans** and is well populated by several species of whales and dolphins, as well as turtles and manta rays. Summer is the season with the highest chance of seeing them, so you can check out one of the associations like **Marelibero** (asdmarelibero.org) and head out to sea on a sailboat – the best way to catch sight of these animals while creating as little disturbance for them as possible.

PISA & NORTHWESTERN TUSCANY

ARCHITECTURE | WILDERNESS | ADVENTURE

Experience
Pisa &
Northwest-
ern Tuscany
online

Hike up to the jagged **Apuan Alps** via Colonnata for spectacular views on the coast and the world's best-known marble quarries (p206)

🚗 *1hr 20 mins from Lucca*

Replenish your vitamin D with a beach break at the WWF-protected Le Dune beach in **Forte dei Marmi** (p217)

🚆 *1hr from Pisa*

Enjoy a sunny day of galleries and top-notch restaurants in the artistic hub of **Pietrasanta** before a sunset swim at the Marina di Pietrasanta (p216)

🚗 *40mins from Pisa*

Lago di Vaglli

Barga ○

○ Colonnata

● **Carrara**

Parco Naturale delle Alpi Apuane

Marina di Carrara

● **Massa**

Marina di Pietrasanta ○

Viareggio ●

Ligurian Sea

Torre ○ del Lago

Lago di Massaciuccoli

Montuolo ○

● **Pisa**

PISA & NORTHWESTERN TUSCANY
Trip Builder

Parco Regionale Migliarino San Rossore Massaciuccoli

First-timers should definitely take a day to explore Piazza dei Miracoli, but thinking that the Leaning Tower is all that northwestern Tuscany has to offer is a big mistake. Go beyond the obvious and discover medieval hilltop towns, rugged peaks and cultural gems yet unspoiled by the crowds.

Le Dune

● **Livorno**

Drive up to **Castelnuovo di Garfagnana** or Barga to explore the farmhouses and rustic hamlets of the region (p214)

🚗 1hr from Lucca

Visit the **Orrido di Botri**, Tuscany's deepest canyon, and trek up a creek among native wildlife (p215)

🚗 1hr from Lucca

Day-trip to lovely **Pistoia** to experience the authentic vibe of this ancient city (p208)

🚆 2hrs from Pisa

Climb Torre Guinigi to admire the well-preserved medieval architecture of **Lucca** from above (p203)

🚆 30mins from Pisa

Discover the white-marble treasures surrounding Pisa's Leaning Tower in **Piazza dei Miracoli** (p196)

🚆 20mins from Pisa Airport

Go truffle hunting in the forests of **San Miniato**, then taste the rare delicacy in an excellent local restaurant (p212)

🚆 1hr from Pisa

Visit the Museo Piaggio in **Pontedera**, the birthplace of Italy's best-known motorised icon: the Vespa (p197)

🚆 20mins from Pisa

E M I L I A - R O M A G N A

Abetone

Bagni di Lucca

Borgo a Mozzano

Margine di Momigno

Montecatini Terme

Prato

Lamporecchio

Arno

Cascina

Montopoli

La Serra

Gambassi Terme

Certaldo

N

0   10 miles
0   20 km

Practicalities

FRANTIC00/SHUTTERSTOCK ©

ARRIVING

Air Pisa's Galileo Galilei International Airport is one of Tuscany's main transport hubs with connections to many European destinations via low-cost airlines. The Pisamover train (tickets €5) runs from 6am to midnight between the airport and the city's central station. A taxi to the city centre should cost around €10.

Train Pisa Centrale station connects with Florence and most major cities in northeastern Tuscany, including Lucca, Viareggio and San Miniato.

HOW MUCH FOR A

Espresso
€1

Craft beer
€6

Dish of pasta
€8

GETTING AROUND

Train If you plan to spend most of your time exploring historical cities, public transport will do just fine. Regional trains may not be fast, but they are frequent and affordable. Remember to purchase and validate tickets in advance; check trenitalia.com for schedules.

Driving Reaching countryside or mountain destinations with public transport will be tricky. Train stations are limited and buses do not run frequently between small towns. Driving is the best way to get around and explore rural Tuscany at your own pace. Opt for a smaller vehicle when possible – streets can be narrow and twisting when you exit major urban centres.

WHEN TO GO

JAN–MAR
Cold, rainy, short days, but there are enough museums to keep you warm and dry.

APR–JUN
Probably the best time to visit, although it might still be snowy at altitude.

JUL–SEP
The summer heat leaves you two options – beach days or mountain hikes.

OCT–DEC
The Garfagnana forests turn red in early autumn; cities light up in the lead-up to Christmas.

EATING & DRINKING

With mountains, hills and sea so close to each other, the variety of flavours emerging from this corner of Tuscany couldn't be more diverse. The precious white truffle (pictured bottom) found in San Miniato attracts foodies from all over Italy between September and December, while further north you'll find IGP (protected geographical indication) products such as spelt and Colonnata's marble-cured lard (pictured top), or DOC (controlled denomination of origin) products such as chestnut flour enriching Garfagnana's cuisine. Needless to say, pasta and wine maintain their evergreen presence on restaurant menus all around.

Must-try truffle-based cuisine
Pepenero (p213)

Best craft beer
Mostodolce (p220)

CONNECT & FIND YOUR WAY

Wi-fi Most hotels and restaurants offer free wi-fi, but other than that you're on your own. Activate a prepaid SIM card with data connection for about €20 (depending on the service provider).

Mountain trails Don't rely on Google Maps when hiking. Instead try mapping apps like Wikiloc and Komoot, which allow you to follow trails uploaded by other users and track elevation, distance and moving time.

BUS RIDES

If you take a local bus, make sure you purchase your ticket in advance at a newsstand or *tabacchi* (tobacconist) shop, marked with a T.

WHERE TO STAY

Historic cities are well connected by rail, making it easy to explore art and architecture at a slow pace. For a more bucolic experience, rent a car and immerse yourself in the picturesque northern part of the region.

Town	Pro/Con
Pisa	With a large student population, Pisa's small city centre offers a lively nightlife and good connections to the rest of Tuscany.
Lucca	Small-town vibe, great dining options and quiet nights; most tourists come to Lucca for the day.
San Miniato	A medieval hamlet serving great food and wine, surrounded by lush greenery.
Pistoia	Cheaper than most other art cities in Tuscany and easy to navigate on foot.
Garfagnana	Plenty of *agriturismi* (farm stays) to choose from in the bucolic nature of the north.
Forte dei Marmi	Some of Tuscany's most luxurious beachside hotels are here; go at your own peril.

MONEY

Cards are widely accepted, but always make sure to have some cash with you, especially if you're driving, as some self-service petrol stations may not accept foreign credit cards.

35 Miracle
SQUARE

ARCHITECTURE | SIGHTS | HISTORY

A record-smashing collection of monumental white buildings emerges from Pisa's red rooftops: surrounding the Leaning Tower is an open-air collection of structures like no other. Go beyond the city's best-known icon and you'll soon find that Piazza dei Miracoli is not just for the architecturally inclined.

WESTEND61/GETTY IMAGES ©

🗺 How to

Getting here If you arrive by train, get off at the closer Pisa San Rossore station rather than Pisa Centrale.

Tickets An all-access ticket (€27) for all the sights in Piazza dei Miracoli is available at opapisa.it. To climb the tower, make sure to book your time slot in advance.

Another icon Visit the birthplace of the Vespa at the **Museo Piaggio** (museopiaggio.it) in Pontedera, 40 minutes by train from Pisa.

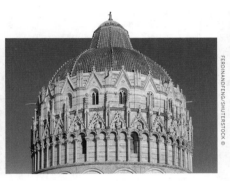

FERDINANDFENG/SHUTTERSTOCK ©

The Bell Tower

Best known as the **Leaning Tower** (Torre Pendente) – a name as creative as the hundreds of pictures taken daily by people pretending to stop it from falling – Pisa's most iconic landmark is a spectacular piece of Romanesque architecture, despite its obvious flaw. Started in 1173 to complete the nearby cathedral, the 56m-tall campanile continues to keep engineers busy after nearly a millennium. Six of the eight floors echo the cathedral's architecture with columns and arches enclosing the cylinder that leads to the top via a spiral staircase. Climb the 251 steps for a close encounter with the bell mechanism and wonderful – although tilted – views of the city.

DIEGO POGGI/SHUTTERSTOCK ©

🖼 Fresco Sketches

During the Camposanto's restoration process many sinopias – the frescoes' preparatory sketches drawn on the walls in red pigment – emerged in nearly perfect conditions. Today these are exhibited in the **Museo delle Sinopie**, which offers a glimpse into the technique of artists such as Veneziano, Aretino, Gozzoli and Gaddi.

Above left Duomo (p198) and Leaning Tower **Above right** Battistero di San Giovanni (p199) **Left** Ceiling, Duomo

Duomo di Pisa

Dedicated to Santa Maria Assunta, the majestic marble construction standing in the middle of Piazza dei Miracoli is a testament to the era in which Pisa was one of Italy's most powerful maritime powers. The facade alternates four blind arches with the three doors which allow entry to the five naves that compose the building which introduced the world to the Pisan Romanesque style.

As you enter, look on your left, where a large Latin epigraph on one of the blind arches tells the story of the cathedral's foundation: in 1063 Pisa's fearsome fleet commanded by Count Giovanni Orlandi attacked Palermo, in Sicily, and sacked the city bringing back six ships full of precious goods and materials – enough to finance the Duomo's construction.

🏰 Why is it Leaning?

In 1178, after five years of construction, the architects working on Pisa's bell tower noticed something was off. Four floors had been built, but it was clear that the structure was leaning slightly northward. The mixture of sand and clay composing the soil under the tower – which would come to weigh 14.5 tonnes – was less than ideal to support the building. Work resumed in 1272, with a new generation of architects attempting to compensate for the lean – perhaps too successfully, since once they reached the 7th floor, they realised the tower was leaning southward (as it is today).

The project was eventually finalised in 1370, but the tower didn't stop tilting until the 1990s, when a technique known as 'controlled sub-excavation' allowed for the tower's foundation to be finally stabilised.

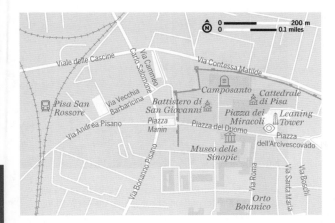

Left Leaning Tower **Below** *Il Trionfo della Morte* by Buonamico Buffalmacco, Camposanto

Battistero di San Giovanni

The circular structure standing in front of the cathedral's western facade is the world's largest baptistery, with a circumference of 107m. The harmonious addition to the Duomo was completed over the course of two centuries starting from 1153 and combines Romanesque and Gothic elements. Enter to see the marble pulpit designed by Nicola Pisano in 1260 and experience the mesmerising acoustic effects produced by the double dome forming the internal roofing system – the staff gives live demonstrations approximately every 30 minutes.

Camposanto

Locked within marble walls, the monumental cemetery founded in 1277 to house the remains of the city's most prominent figures – often recycling precious Roman sarcophagi – used to be adorned with 1200 sq metres of marvellous frescoes authored by the likes of Buonamico Buffalmacco, Taddeo Gaddi and Benozzo Gozzoli. On 27 July 1944, a US grenade set the cemetery's roof on fire, causing massive damage to the paintings that were left exposed to the elements. An attempt to restore the frescoes began in 2009 – after nearly a decade Buonamico Buffalmacco's *Il Trionfo della Morte* (The Triumph of Death; 1336–41) has reappeared in its original location.

An Anarchists' Bastion

MORE THAN MICHELANGELO'S MARBLE: HOW CARRARA BECAME A HOTBED OF RADICAL IDEAS

After the violent suppression of the socialist-inspired Sicilian workers' movement by the Crispi government, a new wave of proletarian political activity began taking shape in the area surrounding the Apuan Alps at the end of the 19th century.

Above left and middle Marble quarries, Carrara **Right** Monument to Alberto Meschi, Piazza Gramsci

FLAVIO VALLENARI/GETTY IMAGES ©

The period following the unification of Italy in 1861 overlapped with the formation of the International Workingmen's Association, also known as the First International, which promoted the collaboration of various leftist groups in the attempt to free workers from class oppression. The radical ideas circulating at the time caught on particularly well in northeastern Tuscany, where masses of *cavatori* (miners) performed an extremely dangerous job – manually extracting massive blocks of marble from the mountains – and spent weeks on end away from their families. Death and injuries were frequent, but the expansion of the marble industry – run mostly by wealthy local families – seemed unstoppable.

Influenced by anarchist thinkers like Carlo Cafiero, a friend of Mikhail Bakunin, and young revolutionary Errico Malatesta, Carrara's quarrymen called for a mass strike on 13 January 1894 to demand better working conditions and in support of Sicilian workers recently besieged by the government's armed forces. The first Italian mass anarchist uprising did not end well – the government of Prime Minister Francesco Crispi arrested over 450 people, with more than 2000 years of collective prison sentences. In the same year, following the attempted murder of Crispi by the hand of anarchist Giovanni Paolo Lega, the government introduced a series of 'anti-anarchist emergency laws' that forced all radical political organisations to dissolve.

Such antagonism, however, made anarchist sentiments in Carrara develop even stronger roots and, ultimately, helped gain some of the rights long demanded by marble workers. In 1911, for instance, anarchist and head of the

Carrara Chamber of Workers Alberto Meschi – whose monument now stands in Carrara's Piazza Gramsci – succeeded in reducing the working day of the *cavatori* to 6½ hours, compensating for the long journeys needed to reach the remote quarries. The first official Congress of Anarchists took place in Carrara after the war in 1945, setting the foundation for the still active Federazione Anarchica Italiana (FAI), whose local headquarters are found in Piazza Matteotti.

> ### The first official Congress of Anarchists took place in Carrara in 1945, setting the foundation for the still active Federazione Anarchica Italiana.

Red and black flags with a circled A are still seen blowing in the wind in Carrara and surroundings, while about 13,000 people continue to be involved in marble extraction, which remains the main driver of the local economy. Much has changed over the course of the past century but the marble industry remains a major cause of concern for the Carrarese community. Since 2005, more than 1200 workers have been injured and 12 have died extracting the 'white gold' from the 165 quarries in Carrara and surroundings which are controlled by fewer than 50 companies – including the Bin Laden family who spent €45 million in the purchase of a concession fee in 2014, becoming the largest foreign investor in the area. As the huge profits made by the few who export the marble once used by Michelangelo and Canova disappear from the town, many wonder what will be left besides debris-polluted waterways, once the landscape is carved empty.

⊚ Anarchic May Day

May Day is a widely celebrated national holiday in Italy (with Europe's largest free music concert held in Rome) and Carrara makes no exception. Since 1946 the city celebrates its own version of May Day, known as Primo Maggio Anarchico. Hundreds of people from Carrara's surroundings reach the town to march through the historical centre from Piazza Battisti to Piazza Matteotti holding red and black flags up in the sky, calling for the end of work rather than the right to work.

36 Medieval **LUCCA**

HISTORY | ARCHITECTURE | DAY TRIPS

Lucca is one of the few urban centres that maintained its independence up to the 19th century. Its historical core has stood the test of time, allowing visitors to get a close encounter with its blend of medieval and Renaissance architecture locked within its city walls.

Above View from Torre Guinigi
Right Statue of Archangel Michael, Chiesa di San Michele

DALIU/GETTY IMAGES ©

🗺 How to

Getting here Lucca is a perfect day trip from both Florence and Pisa. Frequent trains take around 1½ hours and 30 minutes respectively.

Getting around The Porta San Pietro gate is a five-minute walk from the train station. Once you enter, you can reach all the main sights by foot.

Top tip Bookworms will enjoy **Piazzetta dei Libri**, a little square near Via Cenami where street stalls sell secondhand books, comics, prints and rare volumes.

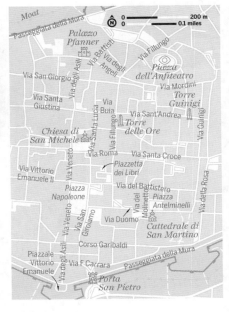

Sublime Cathedrals

Lucca is known as 'the city of a hundred churches', and while even hardcore Catholics might find this overwhelming, it is worth exploring some of the city's best examples of religious architecture. The **Cattedrale di San Martino** (museocattedralelucca.it), originally built in 1070 and continuously transformed up to 1635, blends Romanesque and Gothic elements. Inside, you'll find paintings including Domenico Ghirlandaio's *Sacra Conversazione* (1484–86) and Tintoretto's *Ultima Cena* (1592–94).

Not far away is the **Chiesa di San Michele**, dating back to 795 and located in the heart of the city where the Roman Forum once stood. Look up to see the 4m-tall statue of Archangel Michael atop the marble facade, then enter to admire Filippino Lippi's *Pala Magrini* (1483).

Climbing Torre Guinigi

In the past, over 250 towers built by powerful families to affirm their social status were competing for air space with the churches' bell towers. Today one of the last medieval towers still standing in the city is the 45m-tall

Torre Guinigi (Via Sant'Andrea 41), a structure topped by a garden with 500-year-old holm oaks that belonged to the family of merchants turned politicians of the same name. Climb up the 230 steps (tickets €5) for a 360-degree view of the city. If your thirst for views is not satisfied, head over to the **Torre delle Ore** (Via Fillungo; tickets €5) clocktower and earn another picture-perfect perspective by climbing another 207 steps.

Piazza dell'Anfiteatro

As the name suggests, the elliptical square that marks Lucca's centre was built on the remains of a Roman amphitheatre which attracted up to 10,000 spectators to watch gladiator games. Erected between the 1st and 2nd century CE, the original structure fell out of use with the decline of the Roman Empire, gradually being substituted with new buildings throughout the Middle Ages. In 1830

🏛 Palazzo Pfanner

Leave the imposing medieval architecture behind and enter the gracious atmosphere of **Palazzo Pfanner** (Via degli Asili 33), the 17th-century Baroque residence known for its beautiful Italian gardens designed by architect Filippo Juvarra. This luxurious palace, once the home of Austrian beer brewer Felix Pfanner (1818–92) and Lucca's mayor Pietro Pfanner (1864–1935), has formed the backdrop of numerous movies, including Jane Campion's *Portrait of a Lady* (1996), starring Nicole Kidman and Viggo Mortensen. It's open from April to November (tickets €6.50).

ORIETTA GASPARI/GETTY IMAGES ©

MASCI GIUSEPPE/AGF/UNIVERSAL IMAGES GROUP VIA GETTY IMAGES ©

Lucca Comics & Games

Each October, Europe's largest comics and gaming festival takes place in the heart of Lucca. A weekend filled with events attracts comics enthusiasts and cosplayers from all over Italy, who gather here to attend conferences, markets and exhibitions. See luccacomicsandgames.com.

the architect Lorenzo Nottolini ordered the demolition of the structures that had risen from the arena's foundations, transforming the ancient stadium into the one-of-a-kind oval piazza we see today.

Walk (or Run) the City Walls

Lucca's largest park is also one of Europe's best-preserved fortification structures. The 12m-tall monumental walls surrounding the historical centre have remained intact since their construction in the 16th and 17th centuries. Today they are mostly covered in a green blanket of grass cut by a 4km-long pathway, offering panoramic views of both the city landmarks and the surrounding mountains. If you feel like sweating off some holiday indulgence, join the free **Mura di Lucca Parkrun** (parkrun.it/muradilucca), a 5km community run around the city starting every Saturday at 9am from Piazzale Vittorio Emanuele.

BOTOND HORVATH/SHUTTERSTOCK ©

Left Gardens, Palazzo Pfanner
Top Piazza dell'Anfiteatro **Above** Cattedrale di San Martino (p203)

37 Hike the Apuan
ALPS

HIKING | OUTDOORS | STREET ART

The remote Parco Naturale delle Alpi Apuane offers a seemingly infinite network of trails winding their way through rugged peaks and untamed nature. But that isn't all that the Apuan Alps have to offer. The cultural importance of this area dates back to the Renaissance, when great artists came here to seek the precious white gold in the quarries that continue to shape Carrara's skyline.

NICOBERNIER/GETTY IMAGES ©

🗺 How to

Getting here The easiest way to get to Colonnata, the access point to the trails, is by driving the twisted road that connects it to Carrara (20 minutes). Alternatively, take the hourly bus L50 from Carrara's hospital.

Hiking Trails in the area are managed by the Ital-ian Alpine Club (CAI) and are recognisable by the red and white markers. Maps are available at caicarrara.it and GPS tracks are easily found on major hiking apps.

Hungry? Stop at **Lard Rock Café** in Colonnata for a sandwich with the local speciality, *lardo* (cured fatback).

WESTEND61/GETTY IMAGES ©

Top left Via Vandelli **Bottom left** Hikers, Apuan Alps

Hitting the trails The tiny hamlet of **Colonnata**, known for the production of traditional marble-cured fatback, is the starting point for many trails that climb up to the ridge of the mountains. A great day hike option is to follow route 195, an 8km circular track that reaches 1020m altitude at its highest point and takes around five hours (with breaks) to complete. First take the trail to Cima d'Uomo, then reach Foce Luccica and continue all the way to the ancient Vergheto settlement. Cross the lush walnut forest to Monte Tamburone via route 196 and then head all the way up to Cima di Gioia, where the impressive rainbow *David*, painted by Brazilian street artist Eduardo Kobra in 2017, will appear looking out to the marble quarries.

Marble quarries As you reach a certain altitude you'll soon notice a group of white, severed peaks sitting on the left, between you and the Tyrrhenian Sea. These are just some of the 165 active Carrara marble quarries that have been changing the Apuan Alps landscape for 2000 years. Sections of the (now protected) hiking trail are composed of a centuries-old *via di lizza*, an old track used by miners to slowly slide marble blocks on wooden beams down to the valley, prior to the advent of trucks and modern machinery. It has been estimated that, as a result of technological advancement, more marble has been mined in the past 30 years than in the previous 2000 – the chiseled ridges visible in the distance make the Anthropocene feel terribly real.

Best Hikes in the Apuan Alps

Monte Forato Starting from Fornovolasco this day hike leads to a natural arch that forms a hole in the mountain.

Sentiero dei Ducati A 160km trail across two regions connecting the Apennines with the Apuan Alps through ancient castles and stone villages. Plan through sentierodeiducati.it.

Monte Sagro Expect 360-degree views of both mountains and the ocean from this 1753m peak above Carrara.

Via Vandelli More castles and ancient fortifications along this long-distance trail starting from Modena and ending in Massa, crossing a 172km 18th-century trade route.

38 Charming **PISTOIA**

CITY WALK | HISTORY | ARCHITECTURE

▬▬▬▬ Named the Italian Capital of Culture in 2017, the pleasant town of Pistoia is easily reached from Florence or Pisa making it a perfect day trip away from the crowds. Walk between piazzas in the gracious *centro storico* (historic centre) hunting for medieval, Renaissance and contemporary art scattered around the city.

ATLANTIDE PHOTOTRAVEL/ GETTY IMAGES ©

🎵 Pistoia Blues Festival

Every July the keenly awaited **Pistoia Blues Festival** (pistoiablues.com) gathers music fans in Piazza del Duomo to listen to Italian and international acts. Miles Davis, Sting, Ben Harper, Alanis Morissette and Frank Zappa are just some of the artists that have taken over the festival's stage since its first edition in 1980. Book accommodation in advance.

🗺 Trip Notes

Getting here From Pisa it's two hours by train to Pistoia. The train station is located just 10 minutes from the town centre.

Good to know At time of research, the Fondazione Marino Marini had yet to reopen after the outbreak of Covid-19. However, the *Miracolo* sculpture by Pistoia's best-known artist can be admired for free in the town hall in Piazza del Duomo. The square also hosts a lively market on Wednesday and Saturday mornings.

Top tip Just outside Pistoia, the Fattoria di Celle hosts the permanent **Gori Collection**, a private environmental art exhibition surrounding a grandiose 15th-century villa.

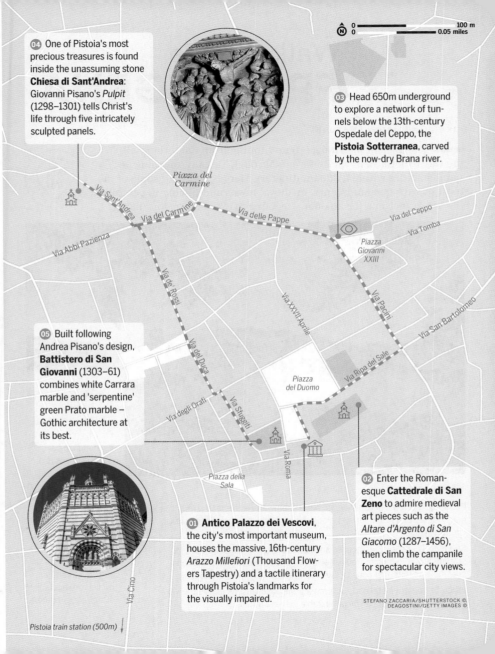

04 One of Pistoia's most precious treasures is found inside the unassuming stone **Chiesa di Sant'Andrea**: Giovanni Pisano's *Pulpit* (1298–1301) tells Christ's life through five intricately sculpted panels.

03 Head 650m underground to explore a network of tunnels below the 13th-century Ospedale del Ceppo, the **Pistoia Sotterranea**, carved by the now-dry Brana river.

05 Built following Andrea Pisano's design, **Battistero di San Giovanni** (1303–61) combines white Carrara marble and 'serpentine' green Prato marble – Gothic architecture at its best.

01 **Antico Palazzo dei Vescovi**, the city's most important museum, houses the massive, 16th-century *Arazzo Millefiori* (Thousand Flowers Tapestry) and a tactile itinerary through Pistoia's landmarks for the visually impaired.

02 Enter the Romanesque **Cattedrale di San Zeno** to admire medieval art pieces such as the *Altare d'Argento di San Giacomo* (1287–1456), then climb the campanile for spectacular city views.

Piazza del Carmine

Piazza Giovanni XXIII

Via Sant'Andrea
Via del Carmine
Via delle Pappe
Via del Ceppo
Via Tomba
Via Abbi Pazienza
Via de' Rossi
Via Pacini
Via San Bartolomeo
Via XXVII Aprile
Via del Duca
Via Ripa del Sale
Piazza del Duomo
Via degli Orafi
Via Stufgti
Piazza della Sala
Via Roma
Via Cino

Pistoia train station (500m)

0 — 100 m
0 — 0.05 miles

STEFANO ZACCARIA/SHUTTERSTOCK ©,
DEAGOSTINI/GETTY IMAGES ©

39 Walk the Via FRANCIGENA

HIKING | RELIGION | NATURE

▰▰▰▰ The ancient pilgrimage route running from Canterbury all the way to Jerusalem via Rome cuts through Tuscany, touching 38 municipalities within a 380km itinerary. Here is a taste of some of the most picturesque landscapes, medieval towns and fascinating culture the Via Francigena has to offer – feel free to extend it to your liking.

STEVANZZ/SHUTTERSTOCK ©

🗺 Trip Notes

Planning Tuscany's official website has a useful interactive map showing stops, guesthouses and water sources along the way. Find it at regione.toscana.it/via-francigena.

Sleeping There are guesthouses and hotels along the route, with prices starting at €30 per night. You will also find pilgrim hostels, churches and guesthouses that offer accommodation in exchange for a donation.

When to go Spring and early autumn are the best seasons to hike the Via Francigena – the heat can be unbearable in the summer.

🚲 Via Francigena by Bike

While much of the Via Francigena is doable by mountain bike, some sections can be difficult to cycle due to uneven ground or steep ascents. An alternative route which avoids such obstacles is marked by blue and white markings. Maps and GPS tracks for cyclists are available at viafrancigena.bike.

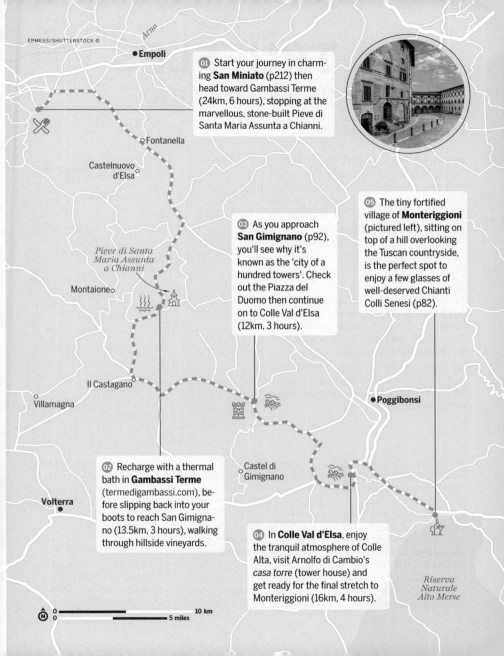

01 Start your journey in charming **San Miniato** (p212) then head toward Gambassi Terme (24km, 6 hours), stopping at the marvellous, stone-built Pieve di Santa Maria Assunta a Chianni.

03 As you approach **San Gimignano** (p92), you'll see why it's known as the 'city of a hundred towers'. Check out the Piazza del Duomo then continue on to Colle Val d'Elsa (12km, 3 hours).

05 The tiny fortified village of **Monteriggioni** (pictured left), sitting on top of a hill overlooking the Tuscan countryside, is the perfect spot to enjoy a few glasses of well-deserved Chianti Colli Senesi (p82).

02 Recharge with a thermal bath in **Gambassi Terme** (termedigambassi.com), before slipping back into your boots to reach San Gimignano (13.5km, 3 hours), walking through hillside vineyards.

04 In **Colle Val d'Elsa**, enjoy the tranquil atmosphere of Colle Alta, visit Arnolfo di Cambio's *casa torre* (tower house) and get ready for the final stretch to Monteriggioni (16km, 4 hours).

ERMESS/SHUTTERSTOCK ©

Arno

Empoli

Fontanella

Castelnuovo d'Elsa

Pieve di Santa Maria Assunta a Chianni

Montaione

Il Castagano

Villamagna

Volterra

Castel di Gimignano

Poggibonsi

Riserva Naturale Alto Merse

0   10 km
0   5 miles

40 TRUFFLES
in San Miniato

FOOD | CULTURE | TRADITION

Visible from a distance, the Torre di Federico II marks the centre of San Miniato, the medieval hilltop town between Florence and Pisa known for its culinary wonders. You can't really go wrong with food here, but if there's one thing you should definitely not miss, it is the local white truffle.

🗺 How to

Getting here San Miniato is 50km from Pisa and 60km from Florence. The train station (San Miniato-Fucecchio) is located in the lower part of town (San Miniato Basso). Take bus 320 to get to the historical centre, 3km away.

Truffle season Different varieties of truffle grow year-round, but the highly prized *tuber magnatum* Pico (white truffle) is found between September and December.

Truffle central As you walk along Viale XXIV Maggio you might notice a small statue of a man patting his dog while holding a heavy clump of gold. It is Massimiliano Benvenuti's wrought-iron **monument to Arturo Gallerini** and his loyal helper Parigi who, in 1954, found the largest white truffle ever recorded, weighing an astonishing 2.5kg. The record-breaking fungus was donated to US president Dwight D Eisenhower, putting San Miniato on the map for food lovers around the globe. Today the **Mostra Mercato Nazionale del Tartufo Bianco** – one of Italy's most important truffle festivals – takes place during the last three weekends of November in the town's historical heart, with stands offering tastings of the freshly hunted delicacy and chefs their interpretation of the edible treasure.

Hunt it yourself Prized white truffles typically grow in calcareous, sloping soils, hiding underground near trees such as oaks, poplars and hazels. Finding them

🍴 Best Restaurants for Truffle

Pepenero Chef Gilberto Rossi presents a constantly evolving, organic-driven menu.

Piccola Osteria del Tartufo Try the truffle honey with cheese, fresh truffle *tagliolini* and truffle mousse.

Le Colombaie All-time classics are enhanced with the exclusive use of regionally sourced ingredients.

Papere e Papaveri A fine-dining experience with an ever-changing seasonal local menu.

is far from easy and San Miniato's *tartufai* (certified truffle hunters) use knowledge passed down through generations to roam forests in search of the right spots to dig. Some of them will allow you to follow along in the hunt – long-time *tartufaio* Massimo Cucchiara organises private truffle hunting tours, taking you along with his dogs in the hills surrounding San Miniato for a truffle hunting session. After a hike in the woods, return to town for a tasting of the freshly collected nuggets. Prices start at €75 per person; book via truffleintuscany.com.

Above Truffle hunting

41 A Wild Garfagnana
WEEKEND

ADVENTURE | OUTDOORS | ROAD TRIP

The valleys formed by the Serchio river are one of Tuscany's richest natural areas – and far different to the picture-perfect hills lined with cypress trees of the south. In the unexpectedly diverse Garfagnana and its surroundings, you can expect deep canyons, rugged mountains, teeming wildlife and lush forests, but also exceptional cuisine, timeless hamlets and medieval fortifications.

ROBERTO FACCHINI/GETTY IMAGES ©

🗺 How to

Getting here The best way to explore Garfagnana is by car. The drive from Lucca to Castelnuovo di Garfagnana via the SS12 takes around an hour.

Ferrovia della Garfagnana An alternative – but slow – way to explore the area is by taking the historical Lucca–Aulla railway; the first section dates back to 1892.

When to go Visit during summer to escape the scorching heat of the large cities and come back during early autumn to see the leaves turning red. Winter and spring get snowy – be careful.

FILIPPO NERI/EYEEM/GETTY IMAGES ©

Top left Rio Pelago, Orrido di Botri
Bottom left Monte Sumbra

Traces of the Middle Ages On your way from Lucca, make a quick stop in **Borgo a Mozzano** to check out the 1000-year-old arched Devil's Bridge, allegedly built by Satan himself. Continue following the Serchio, Tuscany's third river, before making a detour to charming **Barga**, the medieval hilltop village offering exceptional views of the Apuan Alps from the stone-built Collegiata di San Cristoforo. Pick an *agriturismo* to spend the night among chestnut trees or continue to **Castelnuovo di Garfagnana**, the region's main settlement.

Untamed nature From Castelnuovo endless options are available to the adventurous, including mountain biking, rafting and hiking. Head to Capanne di Careggine for a 3½-hour hike to the peak of **Monte Sumbra** (1764m) where spectacular views of the artificial **Lago di Vagli** – which covers the submerged village of Fabbriche di Careggine, abandoned in 1947 – await. For a more chilled experience head to the **Lago di Gramolazzo**; kayaks and pedal boats can be rented at the Camping Lago Apuane.

Caves and canyons If altitude is not your thing, put your speleologist hat on and take a tour of the astonishing **Grotta del Vento** (grottadelvento.com), a 4.5km-long cave featuring rock formations shaped over millennia inside the mountains' belly. Just outside Garfagnana proper, you can also access Tuscany's deepest canyon, the **Orrido di Botri** (open June to September). The 286-hectare reserve surrounding the Rio Pelago is inhabited by squirrels, deer and marmots – follow the creek for 8km amid rocky walls that reach up to 200m high. The trail is as spectacular as it is slippery – hiking shoes and a helmet (available at the entrance) must be worn.

Top Activities in Garfagnana

Mountain biking in the Orecchiella Nature Reserve The trail centre near the Orecchiella Nature Reserve is a spectacular playground for all lovers of the discipline. It's free and is always open (weather permitting). Rental bikes and guides available at garfagnanabike.com

Rock climbing on Pizzo d'Uccello The Oppio-Colnaghi route on Monte Pizzo d'Uccello (1781m) features an 800m vertical wall that has become a mecca for experienced climbers.

Hang gliding over the peaks Flying can be done anywhere in the region – you just have to choose whether you prefer floating over 2000m-tall Apuan peaks or the grassy slopes of the Tuscan-Emilian Apennines.

■ **Alberto Pellegrinetti,** *adventure travel planner* @garfagnanadream.it

PISA & NORTHWESTERN TUSCANY EXPERIENCES

42 Versilia Beach **ESCAPES**

BEACHES | RELAXATION | NIGHTLIFE

From exclusive beach towns populated by celebrities to relaxed stretches of golden sand dotted with colourful umbrellas, Versilia's coast is the ideal destination to recover from wild Garfagnana adventures or a Florentine art overdose. Leave the landmarks behind for a hard-earned Mediterranean summer break.

How to

Getting here Most beach towns can be reached by train from both Florence and Pisa.

Private beaches Most beaches on the Versilian coast are privately run, which means you'll have to rent an umbrella and chairs (starting from €25 per day) to spend the day on the sand.

Free beaches If you'd rather not pay, look for the (very limited) *spiagge libere* (free beaches). The largest in Versilia is the **Spiaggia della Lecciona**, between Viareggio and Torre del Lago.

[Map showing: Marina di Carrara, Massa, Marina di Massa, Parco Naturale delle Alpi Apuane, VERSILIA, Seravezza, Forte dei Marmi, Filippo, Pietrasanta, Marina di Pietrasanta, Mediterranean Sea, Lido di Camaiore, Viareggio, Le Dune (40km), Spiaggia della Lecciona. Scale: 0–5 km, 0–2.5 miles]

Best of both worlds Few places in Italy allow you to go for a hike in the mountains then head to the beach for a swim before the sun sets. **Marina di Massa** is one such place, with long, sandy shores easily reached from the Apuan Alps. Its promenade is an open-air museum of odd statues, including a bronze copy of Michelangelo's *David* and the *Cavallino* statue by Riccardo Rossi.

Art galleries and family-friendly strands Only 3km from the historical centre of **Pietrasanta**, the town founded in 1255 and which boasts the highest concentration of art galleries in Italy, **Marina di Pietrasanta** is one of Tuscany's most beloved

Top right Marina di Massa
Bottom right Beach huts,
Forte dei Marmi

ALESSANDRO COLLE/SHUTTERSTOCK ©

LUCA GRANDINETTI/SHUTTERSTOCK ©

⚜ Viareggio's Carnival

The popular beach resort of Viareggio is known for its lively Mardi Gras party. Spectacular floats depicting actors and politicians parade the streets every February since 1873, attracting up to half a million people to watch massive allegorical constructions of figures. Find out more at viareggio.ilcarnevale.com.

beach towns. Enjoy the chilled atmosphere of the family-friendly, 5km-long sandy beach during the day, then stop at the Pontile di Tonfano to admire the sunset before heading back to Pietrasanta for a lovely dinner at **Filippo** (filippopietrasanta.it).

Beachside glamour Those seeking a glamorous Mediterranean weekend will find themselves at home in **Forte dei Marmi**, a sleepy town with a population of just 7500 that turns into a VIP hive during summer months. The luxurious Twiga club, high-end fashion stores and a long list of 5-star hotels attract ready-to-splurge holidaymakers in July and August. Not feeling very important? Head north to the free WWF-protected **Le Dune beach**, where you'll be able to enjoy both the sea and endemic flora such as sea chamomile and goldenrod without paying €40 for a chair.

Listings

BEST OF THE REST

Surprising Museums

Navi di Pisa Museum

The history of one of Italy's most powerful maritime powers is told through its ancient ships here.

Certosa di Calci

A rich museum of natural history run by the University of Pisa, housed in Calci's beautiful charterhouse founded in 1366 among the Pisan Mountains. Rooms dedicated to zoology and palaeontology sit next to Italy's largest freshwater aquarium.

Museo di Palazzo Pretorio

Prato's most important art museum is housed in a fortification that dates back to the 13th century. See masterpieces by artists such as Donatello, Filippino Lippi and Bernardo Daddi.

Museo delle Statue Stele

Lunigianesi Pontremoli's archaeological museum exhibits a collection of stele statues discovered in the Lunigiana region dating back to the Iron and Bronze Ages.

Museo Leonardiano

The birthplace of Leonardo da Vinci in – you guessed it – Vinci hosts a well-curated museum with one of the largest collections of original documents produced by the artist, plus an exhibition focused on the technologies Leonardo introduced.

Contemporary Art Discoveries

Keith Haring's 'Tuttomondo'

The 180-sq-metre mural Haring painted on the wall of Pisa's Sant'Antonio Abate church was one the last works completed before his death in 1990.

Centro per l'Arte Contemporanea Luigi Pecci

One of Tuscany's most important contemporary art hubs is located in Prato. With a rich exhibition program, cinema, bookshop and live music area, you'll always find something new to stimulate your curiosity. Find out more at centropecci.it.

Palazzo Fabroni

Pistoia's Palazzo Fabroni hosts a permanent exhibition of 20th-century art and rotating contemporary art shows in an elegant building near the Sant'Andrea church.

Peccioli

Despite a population of less than 5000, Peccioli has become a centre of art experimentation that draws visitors from all over Italy. Search for the 'giants' – four monumental statues up to 9m high scattered around the town.

Teatro del Silenzio

Lajatico is best known for being the birthplace of opera tenor Andrea Bocelli. Here the singer created the Theatre of Silence, one of Italy's most picturesque concert arenas, where he holds a yearly festival in July.

DADE72/SHUTTERSTOCK ©

Certosa di Calci

Museo dei Bozzetti

Moulds and sketches by 350 contemporary artists are collected in this little-known museum in Pietrasanta, which shows the creative process behind the production of marble sculptures.

 Outdoor Adventures

Garfagnana Rafting

Kayaking, canoeing, rafting and swimming – immerse yourself in the mountain scenery by trying one of the many water sports possible in the area. Check garfagnanarafting.com for tours and guides.

Monte Forato Swing

A 30m swing mounted at about 1200m altitude on the natural rock arch known as Monte Forato is one of the most thrilling experiences you can have in the Apuan Alps. Contact garfagnanaguide.it to plan the hike.

San Rossore Nature Park

The 23,000-hectare flat, forested expanse near Pisa is a Unesco Biosphere Reserve home to horses, boars, deer and rare plovers waiting to be explored by foot or by bike.

 Authentic Cuisine

Trattoria da Stelio €

This family-run Pisan favourite near Piazza dei Cavalieri has been serving traditional classics at honest prices since the 1960s.

La Ghiotteria €

Generous pasta dishes served on a narrow side street in Pisa's historical centre. Simple, selected ingredients and a no fuss attitude make people come back weekly.

Nanda's €

Lunch spot offering a great selection of vegan burgers, sumptuous stuffed sandwiches and cruelty free first courses in the heart of Lucca.

San Rossore Nature Park

NIK_WILDNAT/SHUTTERSTOCK ©

Osteria dei Cavalieri €€

Expect a charming ambience and top-quality ingredients at this local institution Pisa's Via San Frediano. Best to book in advance, especially on the weekend.

Buca di Sant'Antonio €€

When in Lucca don't miss a dinner at 'La Buca', where the Tuscan tradition comes to life thanks to the detail-oriented yet friendly service and great selection of Colline Lucchesi wine to go with handmade pasta.

Gli Orti di Via Elisa €€

Stylish vibe between Torre Guinigi and Porta Elisa. Local produce sourced from nearby farms makes Lucca's cuisine even tastier. Gourmet pizzas are also available.

Mattarello – Osteria dell'Isola €€

Garfagnana hospitality at its best in a beautiful countryside location below the Apuan Alps with indoor and outdoor seating. Try local specials such as *tagliatelle al farro* (spelt tagliatelle).

Il Pozzo €€

Stop here, in Pieve Fosciana, on your way to Castiglione di Garfagnana for a mouthwatering journey through northern Tuscan flavours. Authentic regional cuisine is cooked following the Slow Food philosophy.

Il Grillo €€

One thing Garfagnana is famous for is its wild game cuisine, and this Giuncugnano restaurant offers exactly that. Spring and autumn are also great for porcini mushrooms – order them fried, you won't regret it.

Osteria dell'Abbondanza €€

A safe bet in Pistoia where tradition takes centre stage with a quiet, warm atmosphere and meat, fish and vegetarian options inspired by 'poor' dishes of the past.

Il Giglio €€€

Located inside an elegant 18th-century palace in Lucca's historical centre, this Michelin-starred restaurant blends exceptional taste with great presentation. Six-course vegetarian tasting menus available.

La Rocca di Castelfalfi €€€

Feeling like a royal dinner? Head to Montaione and try eating in a medieval castle, where Mediterranean flavours are paired with hard-to-beat views of the surrounding rolling hills.

Gelato Hotspots

Il Gelato di Giada

It's worth the trip outside Pisa's historic centre to try the seasonal flavours of artisanal gelato near the university buildings on via Battelli.

Gelateria de' Coltelli

With shops in Pisa and Lucca, Gianfrancesco Cutelli's Gelateria de' Coltelli serves gelati and *granite* with sustainability in mind. Locally sourced fruit is the key ingredient of its seasonal flavours served in recyclable packaging.

Cremeria Opera

Three locations scattered around Lucca make Cremeria Opera impossible to miss. Creative flavour combinations prepared with organic raw materials make memorable frozen experiences.

Craft Beers, Cocktails & Enoteche

Borgo Stretto

Borgo Stretto is one of Pisa's oldest neighbourhoods, formerly a trading spot where merchants would meet in the Middle Ages. Today it's one of the liveliest areas of the city, with bars, pubs and *enoteche* (wine bars) lining up on the street.

La Torre del Luppolo

No better place to go than this informal Via Renato Fucini beer shop in Pisa, offering a large selection of hoppy ales from all over Europe.

Mostodolce

One of Tuscany's best-known brewpubs has its HQ in Prato historical centre, not far from Castello dell'Imperatore. Independently made Belgian- and British-inspired beers on tap – try them all.

Jeffer

This new cocktail bar has quickly become known as one of the best in Pisa. In their latest craft drinks menu titled 'Save the Animals', Jeffer donated €1 for each drink sold to the animal rights organisation Animal Equality.

Borgo Stretto

Bucolic Wine Tastings

Fattoria Sardi

Head out of the city for a wine tasting at this *agriturismo* on the outskirts of Lucca. Visit the vineyards surrounding the picturesque villa, then try the organic reds, whites and rosé produced on the premises.

Maestà della Formica

Three enologists have set up a winery at 1000m altitude on the Apuan Alps, producing a fine riesling on secular vines in the most unusual of places. Book ahead for a tasting at the nearby Rifugio Alpi Apuane.

Podere Còncori

A small, organic winery overlooking the Serchio river, 15 minutes from Castelnuovo di Garfagnana. Tour the vineyards and taste five biodynamic wines (€35 including light bites) in a beautiful rural setting.

Agriturismo Stays

Mulin del Rancone

An old mill turned into a welcoming, family-run farm stay in the heart of Garfagnana. Enjoy the bucolic atmosphere while feasting on cheeses, potatoes and apple pies made in-house.

Borgo del Sole

Four apartments surrounded by the lush forests of the Apuan Alps, best admired in complete silence from the outdoor swimming pool.

Agriturismo Ai Frati

Agriturismo Ai Frati

Set in the historic Convento di San Francesco, a religious structure dating back to 1435, this farmhouse in Pieve Fosciana offers the perfect balance between nature and culture.

Villa Raffaelli

Rustic luxury in a 15th-century villa away from it all, minutes from Castelnuovo di Garfagnana. Come for the splendid views, stay for the glorious food.

Fabbrica di San Martino

The best of both worlds: less than 10km north of Lucca's city centre is this 1751 villa surrounded by greenery where biodynamic wine and olive oil are passionately produced.

 Scan to find more things to do in Pisa & Northwestern Tuscany online

PISA & NORTHWESTERN TUSCANY REVIEWS

DEA / R. CARNOVALINI/ DE AGOSTINI VIA GETTY IMAGES ©

EASTERN TUSCANY

COUNTRYSIDE | CITY WALKS | HISTORY

Experience
Eastern
Tuscany
online

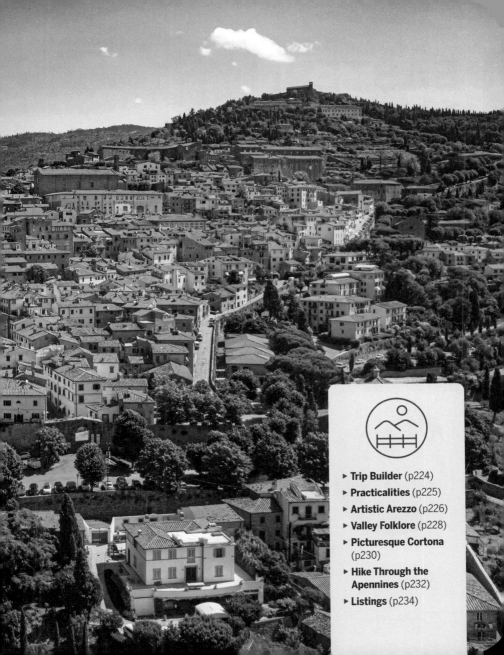

Papiano

Stia

Pratovecchio

Moggiona

Badia Prataglia

Hike up to the peaceful tranquillity of the **Eremo di Camaldoli** (p234)

🚗 1hr from Arezzo

EASTERN TUSCANY
Trip Builder

━━━ Gentle rolling hills, landscapes that seem to have popped out of a painting, centuries of history and colourful folklore – Eastern Tuscany, sitting on the border with Emilia-Romagna, is a countryside fairy tale waiting to prove how real it can be.

Pieve di Santo Stefano

Loro Ciuffenna

Sansepolcro

San Giustino Valdarno

Stop in front of Piero della Francesca's masterpieces at the **Museo Civico** in Sansepolcro (p226)

🚗 40mins from Arezzo

Anghiari

Admire the frescoes inside the Basilica di San Francesco and shop vintage furniture at the Fiera Antiquaria in **Arezzo** (p226)

🚆 1½hrs from Florence

Monterchi

Look over the valley surrounding Cortona at the **Fortezza del Girifalco** (p231)

🚗 40mins from Arezzo

MONDADORI PORTFOLIO/HULTON FINE ART COLLECTION/GETTY IMAGES ©; PREVIOUS SPREAD: ALUXUM/GETTY IMAGES ©

Monte San Savino

Walk through a movie scene in Cortona's **Piazza della Repubblica** (p231)

🚗 40mins from Arezzo

Castiglion Fiorentino

🧭 0 _____ 10 km
   0 _____ 5 miles

Cortona

Practicalities

ARRIVING

Air Florence International Airport is about one hour drive away from Arezzo.

Train The railway station in Arezzo is connected to all major Tuscan cities and the rest of Italy.

FIND YOUR WAY

Tourist offices will usually have paper maps to give out. Digital maps might be inaccurate on isolated country roads or in historic city centres.

MONEY

ATMs are present in major towns, but not always in the countryside. Electronic payments may not be accepted for smaller sums.

WHERE TO STAY

Town	Pro/Con
Arezzo	The major town of the area; can be crowded sometimes.
Cortona	Stay in the town or in one of the *agriturismi* (farm-stay accommodation) in the surrounding hills; having a car is convenient.
La Verna	Stopping at the sanctuary at La Verna is definitely a unique chance; requires adaptability.

EATING & DRINKING

Val di Chiana means *chianina* meat – so if you want to enjoy a good steak, then this is definitely the place to be. To drink, try the sweet wine known as Vin Santo, perfect for desserts; its name comes from its historic use during Catholic Mass.

Must-try pasta
Pappardelle all'aretina
(pictured top; p227)

Best traditional meal
La Bucaccia (p235)

GETTING AROUND

Train Moving on the Regionale line, somewhat slow but cheap, is a great way of admiring the scenery and saving on gas.

Car and bike Rent a car, scooter or bike in Florence or Siena to easily explore the countryside.

EASTERN TUSCANY FIND YOUR FEET

 APR–JUN
Perfect weather for travelling; crowds increase as summer approaches.

 JUL–AUG
High season; beautiful sun but also less-beautiful heat.

 SEP–OCT
Rain is more frequent, but it can still be great travelling weather.

 NOV–MAR
Low season; bundle up against the cold and definitely bring an umbrella.

43 Artistic **AREZZO**

EASTERN TUSCANY EXPERIENCES

HISTORY | CULTURE | CITY WALK

■■■ Sitting at the foot of the Apennines, separating Tuscany from Emilia-Romagna, Arezzo is a photograph of a time long gone. A visit here will take you back to somewhere between the Middle Ages and the Renaissance, when the city thrived and saw the births of some of Italy's most famous writers and artists.

📷 How to

Getting here Arezzo is easily reached by regional train or bus as a day trip out of Florence and Siena.

When to go Late spring and early autumn usually still have lovely weather without the heat of summer.

Vintage bargain If you love hunting for pre-loved furniture and decorative objects, don't miss the **Fiera Antiquaria** (fieraantiquaria.org), which happens every first weekend of the month.

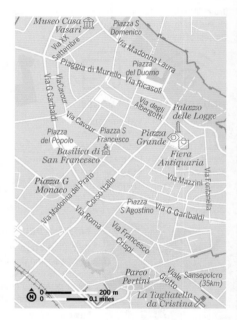

Renaissance art Born in the early 15th century in Sansepolcro, some 30km northeast of Arezzo, Piero della Francesca is universally considered one of the most iconic artists of the Italian Renaissance. To see his works, head to Arezzo's **Basilica di San Francesco**, which holds his famous Storie della Vera Croce frescoes, a series of scenes that narrate the history of the Cross before and after the crucifixion of Christ. The **Museo Civico** in Sansepolcro is also well worth a stop.

Local artist Renaissance painter, architect and historian Giorgio Vasari also hails from Arezzo. He served the Medici for most of his life but also found time to design some work for his hometown. Head to the **Piazza Grande**, Arezzo's main square and the centre of both cultural and social life. On one side of the square,

🍴 Where to Lunch

You can't go anywhere in Italy without finding a local way to serve pasta – and it's no different in Arezzo. Look out for *pappardelle all'aretina* (pasta similar to fettuccine, served with a goose meat sauce) or *tagliatelle al ragù* (another kind of long pasta served with local Chianina meat sauce) on local menus, such as the one at **La Tagliatella da Cristina**. To finish the meal, there's nothing better than a glass of good, sweet dessert wine, better known as Vin Santo, in which to dunk Tuscany's typical *cantucci* – crunchy almond biscuits that need just a little softening in the wine before being perfect to eat.

you'll find the **Palazzo delle Logge**, also known as Logge Vasariane or Logge Medicee, which Vasari designed at the request of Cosimo I Medici. The building echoes the Corridoio Vasariano (p61) at the Uffizi in Florence, which, as the name suggests, was also realised by Giorgio Vasari. To learn more about his life and work, visit the Arezzo home in which he occasionally lived and has been turned into a museum, the **Museo Casa Vasari** (giorgiovasari-ticketoffice.it).

Above Piazza Grande

Valley
FOLKLORE

02

01

03

04

01 Theatre tradition

The *bruscello*, a form of popular Tuscan theatre, takes over Montepulciano each August during the Bruscello Poliziano festival.

02 Target practice

The four neighbourhoods of Arezzo compete each year in the Giostra del Saracino, where riders have to hit the puppet's shield while avoiding its counterstrike.

03 Medieval costumes

The annual Palio horse race in Castiglion Fiorentino is preceded by the magnificent Corteggio Storico procession in which all participants wear historic attire.

04 Spring celebration

Lucignano marks the end of May with its Maggiolata, a weekend filled with flower installations and traditional music.

05 Reenactment

The Battle of Scannagallo, fought in 1554 between Siena and Florence, is brought back to life each year in Pozzo della Chiana.

06 Carnival colours
Carnevale celebrations are a colourful riot, and that's true for the Carnevale of Foiano della Chiana as well.

07 Count's honour
The last days of June see the people of Monte San Savino participating in a series of challenges during the Notte del Conte Baldovino.

08 Take aim
The neighbourhoods of Cortona compete each year in the Giostra dell'Archidado, a medieval-inspired cross-bow competition.

09 Cart race
Valiano is the theatre of the annual Palio dei Carretti, wooden contraptions that zoom down the village's highest hill.

10 Barrel run
Each year people race wine barrels along the streets of Montepulciano during the picturesque Bravio delle Botti.

Picturesque
CORTONA

HISTORY | CULTURE | CITY WALK

▬▬ Inhabited since Etruscan times, the small but mighty Cortona is everything your mind conjures up when you think of delightful Tuscan towns full of history and art. Every cobbled street features an ancient *palazzo* or a typical trattoria, and the rolling hills are an ever-present backdrop. It's the perfect setting for a movie, as Hollywood too has found out.

SIMONA BOTTONE/SHUTTERSTOCK ©

🗺 **How to**

Getting around Car is the best way to see Cortona. The drive from Arezzo is only half an hour and a little under two hours from Florence.

When to go Spring, summer and autumn – but keep in mind that summer means heat and crowds.

Visual art If you're visiting between July and October, stop by the exhibitions of **Cortona on the Move** (cortona onthemove.com), the local festival of contemporary photography.

DEAGOSTINI/GETTY IMAGES ©

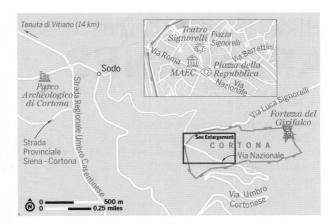

Etruscan remains Cortona was one of the 12 city-states that made up the legendary Etruscan League that so many Roman historians would go on to mention in their works, and the unique archaeological remains here are worth exploring. Start at the **archaeological park** (cortonamaec.org/it/il-parco -archeologico), where you can walk through what remains of the Etruscan city and necropolis. Afterwards move inside Cortona proper and head to the **MAEC** (cortonamaec.org), the local Etruscan museum which collects all the artefacts found in the town's area from the 19th century until today.

Eagle's view Another piece of Cortona's history is the **Fortezza del Girifalco** (fortezzadelgirifalco.it), built during the Renaissance by order of Cosimo I Medici. What was a military construction in the 16th century has become an area for exhibitions and cultural events, and as the highest point in the entire town, it's especially worth a visit for the spectacular eagle's-eye view over Cortona and the rest of the valley.

Cinematic corners Such a picturesque town couldn't remain hidden from Hollywood's eye for long. Quite a number of movies have been shot in Cortona, and walking along the town's historical centre, between the **Teatro Signorelli** and the **Piazza della Repubblica**, you'll see corners that have appeared in *Life Is Beautiful* and *Under the Tuscan Sun*.

Top left Piazza della Repubblica
Bottom left Etruscan amphora, MAEC

Agriturismi Near Cortona

If you want to indulge in a farm stay at a typical Tuscan *agriturismo*, the area around Cortona might just be what you're looking for. Given the town's history as a favoured holiday destination for the rich and powerful of all eras, magnificent villas turned *agriturismi* (or reception halls for events like weddings and birthdays, in case you're brainstorming) dot the surrounding hills. At the **Tenuta di Vitiano** (tenutadivitiano. com), whose main building dates back to the 18th century, you'll be able to hit your daily steps strolling up and down the property's park.

Hike Through the
APENNINES

OUTDOORS | NATURE | TREKKING

The Parco Nazionale delle Foreste Casentinesi stretches along the Apennines that separate Tuscany from Emilia-Romagna. Following its many hiking routes you'll discover villages tucked into mountainsides, remote churches hiding in the middle of the woods and, of course, delicious local food.

MASSIMO SANTI/SHUTTERSTOCK ©

🗺 Trip Notes

Getting here Either car, train (stations like Pratovecchio and Stia) or bus (with Etruria Mobilità and Autolinee Mugello Valdisieve).

When to go Late spring and early autumn are your best chance at pleasant weather without the excessive heat of high summer.

Top tip The Apennines aren't as high as the Alps, but you can still enjoy winter sports at ski areas like the one on **Monte Amiata** (amiataneve.it).

🍴 Mountain Delights

Local cuisine is filled with earthy, flavour-rich specialities like the *gota*, made from pork cheek; cheeses like Tuscan *pecorino* and Raviggiolo; hot slab-cooked *tortelli* and the *melata d'abete* honey. Find out where you can enjoy them all on the website of the **Oltreterra association** (oltreterra.it/gli-operatori).

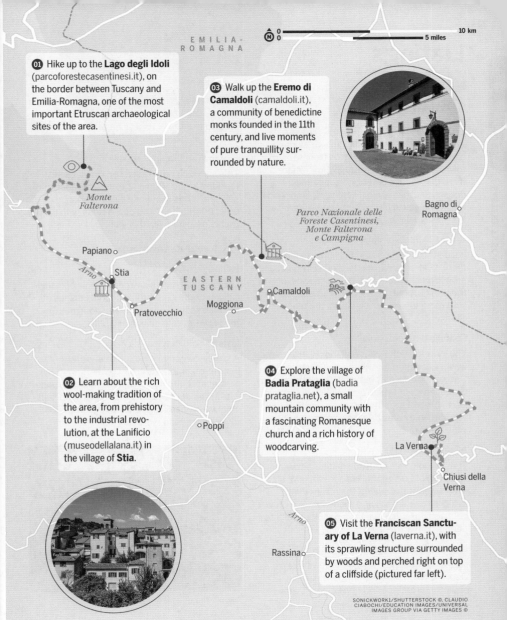

EMILIA-ROMAGNA

N 0 | 0
0 | 5 miles | 10 km

01 Hike up to the **Lago degli Idoli** (parcoforestecasentinesi.it), on the border between Tuscany and Emilia-Romagna, one of the most important Etruscan archaeological sites of the area.

03 Walk up the **Eremo di Camaldoli** (camaldoli.it), a community of benedictine monks founded in the 11th century, and live moments of pure tranquillity surrounded by nature.

Monte Falterona

Bagno di Romagna

Parco Nazionale delle Foreste Casentinesi, Monte Falterona e Campigna

Papiano

Arno

Stia

EASTERN TUSCANY

Camaldoli

Moggiona

Pratovecchio

02 Learn about the rich wool-making tradition of the area, from prehistory to the industrial revolution, at the Lanificio (museodellalana.it) in the village of **Stia**.

04 Explore the village of **Badia Prataglia** (badia prataglia.net), a small mountain community with a fascinating Romanesque church and a rich history of woodcarving.

Poppi

La Verna

Chiusi della Verna

05 Visit the **Franciscan Sanctuary of La Verna** (laverna.it), with its sprawling structure surrounded by woods and perched right on top of a cliffside (pictured far left).

Rassina

Arno

Listings

BEST OF THE REST

◎ Unmissable Sights

Duomo di Arezzo

The Duomo di Arezzo, also known as the cathedral of the Sts Peter and Donato, is the town's chief place of worship, built where the old acropolis probably stood. It also houses another one of Piero della Francesca's masterpieces, a fresco depicting a life-sized Mary Magdalene.

Chiesa di San Domenico

Inside the Chiesa di San Domenico in Arezzo there's yet another masterpiece of Italian art: a wooden crucifix painted by Cimabue, one of the most prominent medieval artists and also, according to popular tradition, the teacher of Giotto.

Castello dei Conti Guidi

The symbol of the village of Pioppi, the castle was the location for the medieval battle of Campaldino, fought between Guelphs and Ghibellines – in which Dante Alighieri took part as well. From the top of the castle's tower you can enjoy amazing views over the entire valley below.

Albero dell'Amore

The 'tree of love', housed inside the town museum of Lucignano, is an impressive sight even without the legend that comes with it. More than 2m tall and made entirely of gold and coral, it is said to bring good luck to people who are in love.

Caprese Michelangelo

As the name might suggest, the village of Caprese Michelangelo is where painter, sculptor, architect and one of Italy's great-est artists Michelangelo was born in 1475. You can visit his house-museum and wander around the same streets he probably walked as a young boy.

Eremo Francescano Le Celle

This sanctuary of Franciscan monks was founded in the Middle Ages by St Francis himself, and it has remained since then a place of quiet mindfulness and community with nature that is definitely worth a visit.

✗ Local Restaurants

La Lancia d'Oro €€€

Located in Arezzo's city centre, this eccentri-cally decorated restaurant serves dishes at the intersection of typical and gourmet. Try the *tagliolini* with seasonal truffle.

Osteria da Giovanna €€

A family-owned business and another Arezzo institution, the Osteria da Giovanna will delight you with its homemade dishes, made with years of experience. Try the *crostini* with chicken liver sauce or the spinach and ricotta ravioli and see for yourself.

Duomo di Arezzo

La Loggetta €€

Looking out onto Cortona's Piazza della Repubblica, La Loggetta restaurant will allow you to enjoy all the best Tuscan culinary tradition has to offer while basking in the medieval vibe that permeates Cortona.

La Bucaccia €€

Located inside a historical palace in Cortona, La Bucaccia carefully curates a menu made of seasonal and locally sourced specialities. That's particularly true for its *chianina*, cured meats and cheeses.

La Loggetta

Fett'Unta Fiaschetteria €€

This *fiaschetteria* (wine bar) is nestled right in the heart of Cortona and is ready to welcome you with all the charm of a traditional Tuscan eatery. Pick one of its seasonal dishes or opt for a carefully selected tasting to discover all that's great about Tuscan cuisine.

La Dogana Enoteca €€

When in Tuscany, you can't go wrong with an *agriturismo* immersed in nature. Valiano's La Dogana Enoteca is the place to sip on a glass of Montepulciano DOC while trying all kinds of local specialities.

Quick Snacks & Sips

Pasticceria Fratelli Bruschi €€

Open since the 1930s in Arezzo, the Pasticceria Fratelli Bruschi serves one of the city's typical desserts: the *gattò all'aretina*, a rolled-up cake dunked in liquor and filled with crème patissière and chocolate cream.

Biancolatte €€

Cheese lovers assemble! Arezzo's Biancolatte is the place to try delicious boards filled with a wide array of cheeses, both local and not, served with jams that help bring out their unique flavours. It's perfect for a quick meal, an *aperitivo*, lunch or anything in between.

Sottopiazza €€

Head to the small Sottopiazza brewery in Arezzo after a satisfying dinner to enjoy a couple more drinks before hitting the pillow. Occasionally you get your beer with a side dish of live music.

🎭 Festival Extravaganza

Incantaborgo

Every July the streets of the centre of Sinalunga fill with wandering artists, putting up plays, musical numbers and performances of all kinds. A great way to enjoy art while also discovering all of the town's hidden corners and streets.

I Giorni dell'Olio Nuovo

Castiglion Fiorentino dedicates an entire weekend to olive oil at the end of November, which is when the *olio nuovo* (new oil) has been pressed and stored away. Restaurants create special menus that prominently feature olive oil, and chances for a tasting pop up at every corner.

 Scan to find more things to do in Eastern Tuscany online

Practicalities

ARRIVING

238

GETTING AROUND

240

SAFE TRAVEL

242

MONEY

243

ACCOMMODATION

244

RESPONSIBLE TRAVEL

246

ESSENTIALS

248

LANGUAGE

250

Right Santa Maria della Scala (p103), Siena

EASY STEPS FROM THE AIRPORT TO THE CITY CENTRE

Tuscany has two main entry points: Florence and Pisa. Both airports are located close to the respective city centres, with frequent public transport connections. Pisa International Airport (Galileo Galilei) is serviced by many low-cost airlines and has double the passenger traffic than Florence Airport (Aeroporto di Firenze-Peretola). It's common to reach Florence via Pisa – a one-hour direct train ride connects them. High-speed trains also reach Florence from most major Italian cities.

AT THE AIRPORT

Arrivi Arrivals

MITCH DIAMOND/GETTY IMAGES ©

SIM cards
You can purchase prepaid Vodafone SIM cards at Forexchange stores found in both Pisa and Florence airports, although it will be significantly cheaper to do so once you reach the city centre. TIM, Vodafone and Iliad all offer prepaid plans starting from around €20.

Currency
Forexchange also offers currency exchange services, although rates are typically better in the city centres. In Florence the store is located in the arrivals hall, while in Pisa you'll find one in the arrivals and departures halls. It's open seven days a week, 8.30am to 8.30pm in Florence and 8.30am to 10pm in Pisa.

Wi-fi Free wi-fi is provided throughout both the Florence and Pisa airports. Just connect to the 'AirportFree WiFi' network to start browsing.

ATMs Known in Italy as *bancomat,* ATMs are available at the arrivals halls in both Florence and Pisa and accept most foreign bank cards.

Charging stations There are type L, 230V power sockets scattered around the waiting halls in both airports, but no proper charging stations.

CUSTOMS REGULATIONS

Cigarettes and alcohol You are not allowed to enter the EU with more than 200 cigarettes, 1L of alcohol with an ABV above 22%, 4L of wine or 16L of beer.

Cash limits When entering or leaving the EU you must file a declaration if you are carrying more than €10,000 in cash.

GETTING TO THE CITY CENTRE

Florence The easiest and cheapest way to get from Florence Airport (Aeroporto di Firenze-Peretola) to the city centre is by taking the T2 tram on the left side of the arrivals hall. The tram runs every few minutes to the Santa Maria Novella train station. Tickets cost €1.50.

Pisa A monorail service known as Pisamover connects Pisa International Airport with Pisa Centrale, the city's main train station, in about five minutes. Tickets cost €5 and can be purchased at the vending machines by the station, steps away from the arrivals hall.

Train The two cities are also connected by a regional train, running between Pisa Centrale and Santa Maria Novella in Florence throughout the day in under one hour. Tickets start at €8.70 and can be purchased directly at the station or online at trenitalia.com.

HOW MUCH FOR A

T2 Tram
€1.50
20mins

Pisamover
€5
5mins

Train (Pisa to Florence)
€8.70
1hr

Taxi You'll find the pickup areas just outside the arrivals terminals of both airports. A €3 surcharge applies during weekends and holidays.

Shuttle bus A shuttle bus connects Pisa International Airport to central Florence and vice versa in approximately one hour. Tickets can be purchased at the airport in Pisa or online at skybuslines.it.

TUSCANY ARRIVING

OTHER POINTS OF ENTRY

Bologna Airport Many low-cost airlines, including Ryanair, Wizz Air and Vueling, fly to Bologna's Guglielmo Marconi Airport (BLQ), located about 100km from Florence. The Marconi Express train (tickets €9.20) runs from the airport to Bologna's central station in seven minutes. From Bologna Centrale to Florence's Santa Maria Novella station fast Frecciarossa trains (€22) take under 40 minutes, while slower regional trains take close to two hours, including a necessary switch in Prato. The Appennino Shuttle bus (appennino shuttle.it) connects Bologna's airport with Florence's city centre directly in 1½ hours (tickets €20).

Coach Long-distance buses are among the cheapest ways to travel in Italy and Europe, with Flixbus and Itabus the most active companies in Florence. The main coach terminal in the city is at Villa Costanza, in the Scandicci area, although some buses stop at the more central Piazzale Montelungo, behind the Fortezza da Basso. From Villa Costanza, Santa Maria Novella can be reached in 20 minutes with the T1 tram (tickets €1.50).

Train High-speed trains such as Le Frecce (trenitalia.com) and Italo (italotreno.it) connect Florence to major cities including Milan, Rome, Bologna and Naples. Book ahead for best prices.

TRANSPORT TIPS TO HELP YOU GET AROUND

While a good rail network connects all major historical cities and a vast amount of smaller towns, getting behind the wheel is how you'll get the most out of your Tuscan journey, especially if time is limited and you're looking to explore rural areas at your own pace. This is, of course, if you're ready to face Italian traffic 'rules'.

CAR RENTAL

Major car rental companies all operate in Tuscany, with the largest selection available in Florence. Rates vary depending on season. A credit card and an EU driving license or an International Driving License is required to rent a car in Italy.

INSURANCE

It is compulsory to have insurance against personal and material damage when driving a vehicle in Italy. All car rental companies offer optional (but recommended) *kasko* coverage, a comprehensive insurance that covers all forms of damage, regardless of whose fault it is.

CAR ESSENTIALS

Car rental from €50/day

Petrol approx €1.80/litre

City parking €2/hour

AUTOSTRADE Small country roads offer the best scenery, but when covering longer distances toll roads allow you to shorten the time needed to get from A to B. Collect your ticket at the entrance of the *autostrada,* and keep it until the exit where you'll be asked to pay based on the distance travelled. Calculate approximately €0.075 per kilometre for regular cars.

ZTL A *zona a traffico limitato* (ZTL; limited traffic zone) is an area where vehicles are restricted during certain hours. ZTLs are usually found in the historical centres of Italian cities and only registered vehicles are authorised to enter them when they are active.

DRIVING ESSENTIALS

Drive on the right; the steering wheel is on the left.

In urban centres the maximum speed limit is 50km/h.

Your car's position lights must always be on when driving.

The law sets a limit of 0.5gm/L of blood alcohol for drivers.

Don't park in front of signs stating *divieto di sosta* (no parking) or your car may get towed.

ROAD TYPES Generally speaking, roads in Italy are split into three main categories. A *strada normale* is a two-lane road that passes through urban centres and has a speed limit ranging between 50km/h and 70km/h. A *superstrada* is a free, multi-lane state road marked by blue signs, with a speed limit of 90km/h. An *autostrada* is a toll motorway connecting major centres where the speed limit reaches 130km/h.

TRAIN The national rail network connects 181 stations in Tuscany. While delays do occur from time to time, trains offer a cheap and relatively reliable way to explore the region. Tickets for regional trains can be purchased on the same day of departure at any station or online via trenitalia.com. High-speed trains operated by Trenitalia and Italo depart from Florence to major Italian cities – tickets can be significantly cheaper when booked a month in advance.

BUS Autolinee Toscana (at-bus.it) manages the bus network in Tuscany, including urban and suburban connections, which you can find on the website. Long-distance coaches run by Flixbus and Itabus ride between major cities in Tuscany, Italy and Europe.

MOOVIT Moovit is the most reliable app to check timetables of local public transport in Italy. Find real-time updates on bus, train and tram travel within Tuscany, including delays and detours, at moovitapp.com.

KNOW YOUR CARBON FOOTPRINT An economy-class flight from London to Pisa will emit on average 238kg of CO_2 in the atmosphere per passenger. A 500km road trip will release approximately 85kg of CO_2, while the same distance covered by a train will emit under 20kg of CO_2.

Many carbon calculators are available online. We use carbonfootprint.com.

TUSCANY GETTING AROUND

ROAD DISTANCE CHART (KMS)

TUSCANY

	Arezzo	Castelnuovo di Garfagnana	Florence	Grosseto	Livorno	Lucca	Pisa	Pistoia	Prato	Siena
Castelnuovo di Garfagnana	190									
Florence	85	120								
Grosseto	130	220	140							
Livorno	160	90	85	145						
Lucca	140	45	75	175	45					
Pisa	140	60	80	150	20	20				
Pistoia	105	80	40	165	85	40	65			
Prato	90	95	25	155	100	55	80	20		
Siena	60	175	65	70	120	135	115	100	85	
Viareggio	165	65	100	170	45	25	25	65	75	160

SAFE TRAVEL

Tuscany is a safe region to explore independently. Most potential risks are connected to road traffic, where lack of focus, weather and other drivers can provoke incidents. When choosing to experience Tuscany with a car, make sure to be fully aware of Italy's road rules and customs.

SPEEDING Driving above the speed limit is common practice in Italy, especially on larger roads. Road users are warned in advance about speed cameras by signs and GPS devices, making it easy to accelerate between them. Do not try to keep up with traffic and leave the left lane free for drivers attempting to overtake.

ICE & SNOW From 15 October to 15 April, it is compulsory to carry tyre chains with you or to mount winter tyres (provided with rental cars). Narrow, twisting mountain roads can be especially dangerous during colder months, when the asphalt can turn into a slippery surface overnight. Make sure to keep an eye on road conditions and weather alerts at all times.

HEAT Summers are getting hotter each year in Tuscany. Over the past decade, the number of days with temperatures above 30°C has grown significantly and the trend appears to be worsening. Forest fires are a major cause of concern during peak summer months – keep an eye on weather warnings. Stay hydrated and keep out of the sun during the middle of the day.

PICKPOCKETS
Theft can occur in crowded areas. Keep your valuables under check at all times when visiting major tourist hotspots and entering public transport. If you need police assistance, call 112 or 113.

DRUGS
All drugs are illegal in Italy. Getting caught with a dealable amount of drugs can lead to prison sentences from six to 20 years.

HIKING The rugged, rocky trails in the Tuscan mountain chains can be challenging. The most remote routes often lack infrastructure; make sure to prepare adequately and consider going with a local guide.

UEUAPHOTO/SHUTTERSTOCK ©, ANDREA MANCINI/NURPHOTO VIA GETTY IMAGES ©

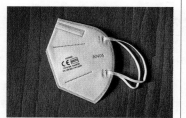

COVID-19 Most of the population in Italy has been vaccinated against Covid-19. At the time of writing, masks are still required on public transport. For detailed info visit salute.gov.it/travellers.

TUSCANY MONEY

CREDIT CARDS According to Italian law, all businesses must accept electronic payments. International cards such as Visa, Maestro and Mastercard are widely accepted, while American Express might be refused in smaller shops and restaurants. Despite this, it is always a good idea to carry some cash for those (rare) vendors who find creative explanations for why their card machines aren't working.

CURRENCY

Euro

HOW MUCH FOR A

Cappuccino
€1.20

Margherita pizza
€7

Glass of Chianti
€4

ATMs Cash machines, known in Italian as *bancomat,* are easy to find in urban centres. Expect charges between €2 and €5 for withdrawals, plus exchange fees if relevant.

VAT REFUNDS
Non-EU citizens spending at least €154.95 in shops displaying a 'Tax Free' sign are entitled to a VAT refund. Find out where to claim your refund at taxrefund.it.

MONEY CHANGERS
Banks often offer currency exchange services to customers only. Unless you have an Italian bank account, you will need to rely on money changers known as *cambia valute,* easily found in tourist areas.

SPLITTING THE BILL There is no fixed rule about splitting the bill in Italy, but splitting *alla romana* (equally among all members of a group) is common practice.

TIPPING
Not expected in cafes, bars and restaurants, unless the service is especially personalised. If you want to leave a *mancia*, rounding up the bill is usually enough.

BUDGET HACKS
With so many delicious local specialities to taste, food expenses can quickly add up. Keep in mind that cafes often charge extra for table service. Save a few euros by having your espresso at the bar, like most Italians do. Hungry? Look out for the many *osterie* and trattorias that offer lunch deals including first and second courses for under €15. When evening comes, seek out *aperitivo* spots that offer finger food with your drink or enjoy some street food – such as *lampredotto* or *schiacciata* – in a public piazza.

DISCOUNTS
Students and seniors have access to discounted tickets at many cultural sights around Tuscany. Consider purchasing the **Firenzecard** (firenzecard.it), which includes access to dozens of museums in Florence for €85 (valid 72 hours). Annual subscription tickets for the Uffizi Galleries are also available for €70 online at uffizi.it.

UNIQUE & LOCAL WAYS TO STAY

TUSCANY ACCOMMODATION

Art cities might get crowded during the high tourism season, but elsewhere you'll soon encounter a vast selection of rural residences ready to welcome you in their bucolic atmosphere. Book an agriturismo (farm-stay accommodation), B&B or a room in a medieval castle to get back in touch with nature and enjoy Tuscany from a relaxing perspective.

HOW MUCH FOR A

Hostel dorm
€35/night

Agriturismo
€80/night

Boutique hotel
€90/night

LISA-BLUE/GETTY IMAGES ©

CASTLE STAYS As you've likely gathered, the Tuscan countryside is dotted with a plethora of medieval fortifications built by powerful families of the past. Many of the castles that had been left abandoned for centuries have been refurbished and turned into luxurious residences that pay tribute to their glorious origins. Castle stays – such as those found in the Chianti area or in the Arezzo province – often feature swimming pools surrounded by sloping vineyards and olive groves and in-house restaurants serving refined local cuisine.

BOUTIQUE HOTELS

Small, independently run hotels with an artistic touch combine welcoming, personalised service with an intimate experience that makes you want to return at the end of a long day exploring. Art cities such as Florence, Pisa and Siena offer the most choice when it comes to cosy yet elegant accommodation.

RIFUGI

Tuscany has a great network of *rifugi* (mountain huts) welcoming mountain lovers (mostly) between April and October. Basic rooms in altitude lodges and simple shelters known as *bivacchi* are managed by CAI, the Italian Alpine Club, and should be booked in advance by calling directly. More info at cai.it.

MYVIDEOIMAGE.COM/SHUTTERSTOCK ©

FANI KURTI/GETTY IMAGES ©

AGRITURISMI Postcard-worthy farm stays are everywhere in Tuscany. Just leave the city behind and head for the hilly countryside to find one of the most relaxing forms of accommodation, located at the intersection between culture and scenery. Far from museum queues and opulent palaces, the region's many idyllic *agriturismi* vary in size, price and services – ranging from family-run B&Bs to sophisticated, old-charm apartments with modern amenities – but they all typically offer an experience centred around the celebration of local produce through scrumptious, homemade meals made to be enjoyed at a slow pace.

Whether it is with organic wine, olive oil, cheese or pasta, surrender to the rhythms of the countryside to get a taste of the rural lifestyle. Farmhouses are not necessarily located in remote areas – if you have a car, you can choose to set up base in an *agriturismo* and explore the region from there, taking day trips to cities and ancient hamlets. Obviously, seasonality plays a major role in the quality of your *agriturismo* stay. Book your trip between late spring and early autumn to get the most of the outdoors and enjoy the fruits of the land at their freshest.

BOOKING

Most accommodation options in Tuscany can be booked through major international booking platforms or by reaching out directly to the property. Prices increase significantly during the high season (April to October) and the period surrounding Christmas. Coastal towns experience their peak influx of tourists in July and August, when the majority of Italians go on holiday. Book well in advance to find the best deals. Note that in most cities you'll be asked to pay a tourist tax on top of the accommodation's price, ranging from €1 to €5 depending on the rating of the property you choose to stay in.

Next to the big booking websites, you should also take a look at these platforms:

Agriturismi.it Search for farm stays in Tuscany (and Italy) and book directly through the owners.

Ecobnb.it Hotels and guesthouses are rated by their level of sustainability.

CAMPING
Free camping is not allowed in Italy, but numerous equipped campgrounds are found along the coast, where you can either pitch your tent or park your van steps away from the beach.

POSITIVE-IMPACT TRAVEL

Tips to leave a lighter footprint, support local and have a positive impact on local communities.

ON THE ROAD

Hire a hybrid or electric car to reduce your emissions during your road trip and seek accommodation options that offer charging stations.

Carpool. If public transport isn't available, use platforms such as BlaBlaCar to share a ride to your destination.

Leave no trace behind. Not all mountain trails are managed regularly, so make sure to bring any trash back with you when hiking.

Cycle. The bending roads that stretch through the hilly countryside are often looked at as a cyclists' heaven. Consider exploring on two wheels to enjoy the views without adding to your footprint.

Avoid single-use plastic. Italy has the highest consumption of bottled water in Europe. Don't fall into this bad habit – tap water is good to drink everywhere.

MASSIMO TODARO/SHUTTERSTOCK ©

GIVE BACK

Volunteer at one of the 17 natural areas protected by WWF in Tuscany. Consider joining the organisation in one of the many initiatives planned throughout the year, including beach cleanups and conservation workshops. Learn more at wwf.it.

Learn about conservation. The Tuscan section of Legambiente (legambientetoscana.it), Italy's largest environmental-protection organisation, holds various events where you can gain awareness about issues related to the preservation of local ecosystems.

Visit dying towns away from the big cities. Many rural settlements have been suffering from significant depopulation and economic decline over the past decades, as younger generations move to the larger cities in search for opportunities. Make sure to exit the tourist trails and get to know the lesser-visited areas of the region.

DOS & DON'TS

Don't expect meals to be served outside Italian lunch (noon to 2pm) and dinner times (7pm to 10pm).

Don't climb, sit on or touch historical monuments present in public spaces.

Do learn a few words in Italian – they will come in handy, especially outside major cities.

Do cover your legs and shoulders when entering churches.

LEAVE A SMALL FOOTPRINT

Skip the Florentine steak. Beef is responsible for the largest release of greenhouse gas emissions compared to other foods. Instead consider the dozens of vegetarian pasta dishes that are available, next to traditional meals such as *panzanella, pappa al pomodoro* and *ribollita*.

Visit less. Rather than trying to squeeze as many sights as possible into your trip, consider spending more time in fewer places to get a better feel for the local lifestyle while cutting your emissions.

Opt for the train. Rail travel can drastically reduce your footprint compared to driving and most urban areas can easily be reached by train.

TUSCANY RESPONSIBLE TRAVEL

CARLINA TETERIS/GETTY IMAGES ©

SUPPORT LOCAL

Slow Food The Slow Food organisation (slowfood.it) promotes restaurants and farms that preserve genuine traditions and local ecosystems. Seek out venues awarded by Slow Food's guide to support the region's biodiversity and the people who care about it.

Mostra dell'Artigianato Buy from local artisans rather than big chain stores. Florence organises the Mostra dell'Artigianato, an international crafts fair, every year in April. Learn more at mostrartigianato.it.

CLIMATE CHANGE & TRAVEL

It's impossible to ignore the impact we have when travelling, and the importance of making changes where we can. Lonely Planet urges all travellers to engage with their travel carbon footprint. There are many carbon calculators online that allow travellers to estimate the carbon emissions generated by their journey; try resurgence.org/resources/carbon-calculator.html. Many airlines and booking sites offer travellers the option of offsetting the impact of greenhouse gas emissions by contributing to climate-friendly initiatives around the world. We continue to offset the carbon footprint of all Lonely Planet staff travel, while recognising this is a mitigation more than a solution.

RESOURCES

legambientetoscana.it
regione.toscana.it/ambiente
wwf.it
slowfood.it

ESSENTIAL NUTS & BOLTS

CHEEK KISSES
On informal occasions, people greet each other giving two light cheek kisses. Alternatively, a handshake or just saying *'Ciao!'* will do just fine.

STREET DRINKING
Drinking on the street is allowed in Italy, although local regulations may impose restrictions in certain areas. Be discreet.

MASS HOLIDAYS
The vast majority of Italians take their holidays in August, so expect beaches to be packed.

FAST FACTS

Time Zone
CET (UTC+1)

Country Code
+39

Electricity
220V-230V/
50Hz

GOOD TO KNOW

Many shops close between 1pm and 4pm to allow workers to take a lunch break.

Smoking inside public places is prohibited everywhere, including restaurants, shops and public transport.

The legal drinking age is 16 in Italy, although there is no limit on who can purchase alcohol at the store.

By law, cash payments are limited to a maximum of €2000.

Cappuccino is considered a breakfast drink. Stick to espresso after 11am.

ACCESSIBLE TRAVEL

Cobblestone streets Old city centres often feature cobbled streets that can be very difficult to navigate in a wheelchair.

Museum access The main museums in Florence are all accessible for wheelchair users. All Florentine Civic Museums provide free priority access for people with disabilities. Visit uffizi.it/en/special-visits/uffizi-by-touch to learn about special tours for people with visual impairments.

Trains and trams All high-speed trains and most regional trains have at least one carriage equipped for passengers who use wheelchairs. Trams in Florence are accessible for people who use wheelchairs.

ZTLs Tourists with disabilities are allowed to access the limited traffic zone in Florence's city centre with their vehicles. A free permit needs to be requested in advance – email upd@serviziallastrada.it with your name, license number and plate number.

VISAS
Tourists from 62 non-EU countries can visit Italy without a visa for up to 90 days.

DRESS TO IMPRESS
Italians care about their appearance (and will judge you accordingly), especially in cities.

PUBLIC TOILETS
Museums and cafes are your best option when it comes to public toilets.

FAMILY TRAVEL

Museums Admission to national museums, galleries and archaeological sites is free for EU citizens under the age of 18.

Tram and train Kids shorter than 1m travel for free on Florence's trams. Train travel is free for children under the age of four, as long as they don't occupy a seat.

Parco di Pinocchio Carlo Lorenzini, better known by his pen name Carlo Collodi, wrote the tale of Pinocchio in Collodi, not far from Pistoia. Here a theme park dedicated to the famous children's story features adventure trails, a museum and a butterfly house for kids. Family tickets cost €60; book at pinocchio.it.

DIGITAL NOMADS An increasing number of laptop-friendly cafes are popping up in Florence, but unless a venue is clearly designed for that purpose you shouldn't occupy a table for hours without buying anything. Co-working spaces charge approximately €20 per day for a desk.

PUBLIC TRANSPORT TICKETS Paper train tickets purchased at the station should be validated before entering the train. Tickets bought online do not need to be validated. Bus tickets should be purchased in advance at newsstands or tobacconists and validated on the bus.

LGBTIQ+ TRAVELLERS
Despite the Catholic influence on local culture, Tuscany is fairly open when it comes to the LGBTIQ+ community. Venues like Il Piccolo (p73) and Queer in Florence and Castigo in Pisa are renowned community hotspots, while the coastal towns of Torre del Lago and Viareggio also have lively scenes.

Florence Queer Festival (florencequeerfestival.it) is Tuscany's main cultural event dedicated to the queer community, showcasing films, art, photography each September.

IREOS (ireos.org), **Azione Gay e Lesbica** (azionegaye lesbica.it) and **ArciGay Firenze** (arcigayfirenze.it) offer counselling and legal assistance in case of harassment.

...velop in the 13th ...rough the works ...ll Tuscans – who ...ct. Although ..., standard Italian is ...ughout the country. The sounds used in spoken Italian can all be found in English. If you read our pronunciation guides as if they were English, you'll be understood. The stressed syllables are indicated with italics. Note that *ai* is pronounced as in 'aisle', *ay* as in 'say', *ow* as in 'how', *dz* as the 'ds' in 'lids', and that *r* is a strong and rolled sound.

BASICS

Hello.	*Buongiorno.*	bwon·*jor*·no
Goodbye.	*Arrivederci.*	a·ree·ve·*der*·chee
Yes./No.	*Si./No.*	see/no
Please.	*Per favore.*	per fa·*vo*·re
Thank you.	*Grazie.*	*gra*·tsye
You're welcome.	*Prego.*	*pre*·go
Excuse me.	*Mi scusi.* (pol)	mee *skoo*·zee
	Scusami. (inf)	*skoo*·za·mee

What's your name?
Come si chiama? (pol)   ko·me see *kya*·ma
Come ti chiami? (inf)   ko·me tee *kya*·mee

My name is ...
Mi chiamo ...   mee *kya*·mo ...

Do you speak English?
Parla/Parli   par·la/par·lee
inglese? (pol/inf)   een·*gle*·ze

I don't understand.
Non capisco.   non ka·*pee*·sko

TIME & NUMBERS

What time is it?	*Che ora è?*	ke *o*·ra e
It's (two) o'clock.	*Sono le (due).*	*so*·no le (*doo*·e)
Half past (one).	*(L'una) e mezza.*	(*loo*·na) e me·*dza*

in the morning	*di mattina*	dee ma·*tee*·na
in the afternoon	*di pomeriggio*	dee po·me·*ree*·jo
in the evening	*di sera*	dee *se*·ra
yesterday	*ieri*	*ye*·ree
today	*oggi*	*o*·jee
tomorrow	*domani*	do·*ma*·nee

1	*uno*	*oo*·no	6	*sei*	say
2	*due*	*doo*·e	7	*sette*	*se*·te
3	*tre*	tre	8	*otto*	*o*·to
4	*quattro*	*kwa*·tro	9	*nove*	*no*·ve
5	*cinque*	*cheen*·kwe	10	*dieci*	*dye*·chee

EMERGENCIES

Help!	*Aiuto!*	a·*yoo*·to
Leave me alone!	*Lasciami in pace!*	*la*·sha·mee een *pa*·che
Call the police!	*Chiami la polizia!*	*kya*·mee la po·lee·*tsee*·a
I'm lost.	*Mi sono perso/a.* (m/f)	mee *so*·no *per*·so/a

Index

000 Map pages

'The statue of Dante in front of Florence's Santa Croce has prompted many rounds of Divine Comedy "verse-offs". Must turn that frown he has upside down somehow.'

BENEDETTA GEDDO

'I took a breather (OK, a nap) on the Orto de' Pecci grass and woke to find a peacock standing close by!'

MARY GRAY

'It didn't take long to realize that cycling in the Chianti region is as difficult as the winemakers you meet are generous.'

ANGELO ZINNA

'All Italian nerds know that Lucca means one thing and one thing only: Lucca Comics & Games. Nothing beats watching a group of Game of Thrones cosplayers taking on a professional photoshoot under the city's Renaissance walls.'

BENEDETTA GEDDO

'Twice I attempted to find what is said to be one of Italy's last remaining anarchist cafes in the tiny town of Gragnana, near Carrara – to no avail.'

ANGELO ZINNA

XSMIRNOVX/SHUTTERSTOCK ©, MESKPHOTOGRAPHY/SHUTTERSTOCK ©

THIS BOOK

Design development
Lauren Egan, Tina García, Fergal Condon

Content development
Anne Mason

Cartography development
Wayne Murphy, Katerina Pavkova

Production development
Mario D'Arco, Dan Moore, Sandie Kestell, Virginia Moreno, Juan Winata

Series development leadership
Liz Heynes, Darren O'Connell, Piers Pickard, Chris Zeiher

Commissioning editor
Daniel Bolger

Product editor
James Appleton

Cartographer
Rachel Imeson

Book designer
Ania Lenihan

Assisting editors
Melanie Dankel, Gabrielle Innes, Gabrielle Stefanos, Saralinda Turner

Cover researcher
Gwen Cotter

Thanks Sandie Kestell, Amy Lynch, Darren O'Connell, John Taufa